To A. S. Kedzie

from

Dr R C Kedzie

With Great Respect

Thence to

Rev. W. E. Caldwell.

Enjoining that, taking in the scope of these Lectures & drinking in their spirit, he therewith innoculate & inspire his people.

GRAHAM LECTURES.

Human Society:

ITS PROVIDENTIAL STRUCTURE, RELATIONS, AND OFFICES:

EIGHT LECTURES

DELIVERED AT THE BROOKLYN INSTITUTE,
BROOKLYN, N. Y.

BY

F. D. HUNTINGTON, D.D.

NEW YORK:
ROBERT CARTER & BROTHERS,
530 BROADWAY.

1860.

STEREOTYPED BY
THOMAS B. SMITH & SON,
82 & 84 Beekman-street, N. Y.

PRINTED BY
E. O. JENKINS,
28 Frankfort-street, N. Y,

GRAHAM LECTURES:

ON THE

POWER, WISDOM AND GOODNESS

OF GOD,

AS MANIFESTED IN HIS WORKS.

VOLUME II.

PUBLISHED BY

THE BROOKLYN INSTITUTE

INTRODUCTORY NOTE.

For the sake of convenience and clearness in the arrangement, what was prepared and delivered as six Lectures, is here, with a few additions, distributed into eight.

F. D. H.

CAMBRIDGE, May 1, 1859.

PREFACE.

THE Directors of the Brooklyn Institute have much pleasure in presenting to the Public, the Graham Lectures, thus far published, on the POWER, WISDOM, AND GOODNESS OF GOD, AS MANIFESTED IN HIS WORKS.

This course, by Professor Huntington, was very fully attended; so much so, as to make it very desirable that we should have a larger room than the present one for the future lectures of the Institute.

These Lectures were intended by Mr. Graham to treat of the works of God, separate and apart from polemic theology, or the peculiar doctrines of the sects into which the religious world is divided.

The whole of God's works may furnish the subjects of these discourses, whether in their greatest or most minute forms; their simple or their complex organizations; their adaptations, their laws, their skill, their wisdom, their harmonies, their divine character. The lecturer, therefore, stands, as it were, in the presence of the great Architect, to expound that portion of the creation which he has chosen for his theme, and thus to exhibit the "Power, Wisdom, and Goodness" of the Creator, as teaching the sublime sentiments of justice and benevolence to all His creatures, and of love and reverence for the Universal Father.

The Directors feel gratified with the success of these Lectures, and shall continue, from time to time, as funds arise from the noble endowment of Mr. Graham, to endeavor to procure the requisite talent and accomplishment for future courses of lectures; such as shall gradually form a series of publications of sterling character, eminently useful, elevating to the public taste and morals, and honorable to our Institute.

PETER G. TAYLOR, *President;*
OLIVER HULL, *Vice President;*
JOHN W. PRAY, *Secretary;*
THOMAS ROWE, *Treasurer.*

THOMAS WOODWARD, WILLIAM EVERDELL, JR.,
AUSTIN MELVIN, DUNCAN LITTLEJOHN,
ELIAS LEWIS, JR., GEORGE KISSAM,
ALFRED M. WOOD, CHARLES H. BAXTER,
JESSE C. SMITH,
Directors.

BROOKLYN, October 1, 1859.

CONTENTS.

GRAHAM LECTURES.

LECTURE I.

SOCIETY A DIVINE APPOINTMENT.

HERE, on the scene of his industrious and beneficent life, among his fellow-citizens who knew his virtues so well, who reap a daily advantage from his liberal foresight, and who honor his memory faithfully, it is not for me, a stranger, to eulogize the man who laid the foundation of these Lectures. When he provided, in his last testament, that their ever-recurring subject should be the Wisdom, the Power, the Goodness of our God, he neither over valued the inexhaustible richness of the theme, nor mistook the first need of his age. Of all his enterprise, his integrity, his success, that thought for his Creator's honor was the crown. In that provision, according to the terms of it, his laborious career rose into the region of worship.

In the particular line of thought through which I

am to attempt to aid in carrying out the noble purpose of the Founder, it is among my satisfactions that my choice falls into an orderly connection with what was so ably and brilliantly presented by my only predecessor in the series.*

The Lecturer who went before me exhibited the illustrations of those Divine Attributes as they lie in the "Constitution of the Human Soul." From that, what so natural as to proceed outward into the attitude and offices of human beings toward each other; to contemplate the wonderful texture, the manifold elements, the living powers of the Social Body; and to trace the marks of a Heavenly Parentage and Providence in the universal association of man with man? Uniting the Founder's general testamentary precept with my own special selection, and giving my whole subject an express statement, it is THE WISDOM, POWER, AND GOODNESS OF GOD AS MANIFESTED IN THE STRUCTURE, THE OFFICES, AND THE RELATIONS OF HUMAN SOCIETY.

It will not be supposed that any formal attempt

* Rev. R. S. Storrs, Jr., D.D., of Brooklyn. The place he occupies in that community will justify the personal reference, if I express the joy I feel in adding to many earlier bonds of attachment between him and me, this coincidence of studies in the common prosecution of one of the most munificent public designs that any single American benefactor has initiated. The Lectures of Dr. Storrs were published by the "Institute" in 1857.

is to be made to demonstrate to a sceptical understanding the fact that there is a God. Not only that primary religious truth, which even Revelation assumes in its first sentence, is supposed to be granted, but many related and dependent truths besides. The real infirmity of Christian faith is not that the being and attributes of the Deity are denied, but that they lie off from the living apprehension of the spiritual nature. Much as we distrust the religious competency of the intellect, the brain does not play, by any means, the worst part in atheism: its most frequent error in that respect is, that it fancies itself an atheist when it is not, but is only playing atheist, at the instigation of pride, or appetite, or disappointed ambition, or some other demagogue in the rabble of the passions. The grand necessity of religion at present, I conceive, is not to find out whether God is, but where he is: that is, to apprehend his immediate activity and Lordship in the world of our life, so joined with it as he could only be through the incarnation. I take one of the departments of that life, lying midway between the individual consciousness or personality and outward nature:—Humanity in its social combinations; and with the twofold object of gaining a rational interpretation of society itself, by investigating it from its only centre, or point of original power, and of showing how it lies perpetually within the conscious presence, and subject to the instant control, of the Infinite Spirit. So far as my inquiries have extended, there is not, in any literature, anything like a systematic or philosophical attempt to trace the laws, or to unfold the significance of Human Society, under this, or indeed any other, very comprehensive principle of analysis and combination. I do not aspire to supply that deficiency. Neither the original purpose of Mr. Graham, nor your own view of what would be most useful, as it seems to me, would lead us here to that more speculative method of treatment, which would be natural if a pure philosophy of the subject were the object contemplated. But you have come together to enter on a study in that direction with me to-night. I cannot help telling you how much it adds to my own interest, beforehand, in the evenings we are to spend together, that, by the continuity, regularity, and frequency assigned to these exercises by the judgment of the "Institute," our assembly takes on something of the character of a domestic circle, where speaker and hearers are constantly coming into a more direct and simple relation with one another, illustrating, in fact, much belonging to the very theme we have to unfold. You will be patient with defects. You will take pains to notice the distribution and mutual connection of the parts. And you will remember how much, both from the necessary restrictions of time, and from limitations more obstinate than those, must be left out.

The lectures will be arranged in the following order of subjects. In the 1st, Society will be considered as a Divine Appointment in itself; in the 2d, as a Living Instrument of Divine Thought; in the 3d, as a Discipline of Individual Character; in the 4th, as a School of Mutual Assistance; in the 5th, as to Social Theories; in the 6th, as a Motive and Incentive to the Intellect; in the 7th, as holding in itself Laws of its own Progression; and in the 8th, as the Sphere of the earthly Kingdom of Christ.

Taking Lord Bacon's division of human knowledge into History, Philosophy, and Poetry, our subject cannot be assigned exclusively to the province of either one, but it touches them all. It opens into History, for, as Dr. Arnold has so well said, "The general idea of history seems to be that it is the biography of a society having a common life." It has to do with Philosophy, for we are to regard this Social Life pre-eminently as under laws, laws that condition and regulate its growth, laws whose wonderful working, from Eden in the past to the mysterious issues of the future, furnish to the philosophic mind its profoundest problem. It includes the source of Poetry, because it is out of the rise and conflict, the ecstacy and suffering, the joy and agony, of those very passions which form the elements of social change, that imagination builds its most august and wondrous visions, and the poet, tragic, lyric, or epic, sings his immortal song.

Remark that Society, as we are here to consider it, is not a society formally organized, combined into a commonwealth, constituted into a political unity. Universal society has not as yet taken that shape. Whether such a sublime consummation is ever to be; whether the nations of the earth are yet to be drawn under a single outward economy, not only moral but civil, and the golden index of old prophecy be seen pointing to a Fold which shall be also a State,—the Law going forth from some central Jerusalem, and all nations flowing into it,—this may be a question for faith, a dream for hope. The principles now to be discussed are independent of that speculation. They stand even in society as it now is, broken, of diverse races, of warring tribes,—a multitude, but not a proper union: inasmuch as beneath all its variety of polities, and all its diversity of culture, and all its hostility of interests, there runs, deep down, a mighty bond of oneness after all, best expressed by the simple word *human*, making each man, despite every difference, brother to every other man; just as one comprehensive principle encircles and pervades all varieties of vegetable production, from hyssop to cedar, or one artistic design winds into a profound harmony all the unequal keys and notes and instruments of an orchestra, and all the measures, themes, voices, and even pauses, of an oratorio. For, as a scholar in the oldest English university* has finely said: "Universal history has enriched our language with a word that never passed the lips of Plato, Socrates, or Aristotle,—the word *mankind.* Where the Greek saw barbarians, we see brethren. Where he saw heroes and demigods, we see parents and ancestors. Where he saw nations, we see mankind many ways severed, but moving to one destiny, and bearing one image of God; as where the ancient astronomic observer saw separate spheres in the sky, we see a single system, balanced in itself and harmonized by one centralizing attraction."

At present, I ask you to contemplate society, under a somewhat introductory and general aspect, as a Divine appointment in itself. And this may be set forth the more clearly, if we seek the proofs, first, in the nature of the thing, Society; secondly,

* A. P. Stanley, now "Regius Professor of Ecclesiastical History" at Oxford, in his Inaugural Address.

in its origin; and thirdly, in its historical development.

I. To know society, either as to its composition or its functions, doubtless we must first know man. Man is the prime material of mankind. Society is simply human nature existing in its natural combinations. It is all the faculties of man in one mode of their exhibition,—reason, will, conscience, affection. Only, consider, the combination is such, that the humanity itself could not be complete without it. There are capacities in man to which society is just as necessary as light to the eye or food to the body. You cannot do your best, put forth your strongest, live out your noblest, save in a social state, where every other man is free to do the same. In one sense, man is greater than society; as the simple personality is greater in itself than in any one of its modes of being and acting. Yet, society is a grander interest than the interest of any one man. If there must be a conflict of rights or privileges, those of many are dearer than those of one. But, when we come to duties, or *the right*, the collision is an impossibility. No public duty can be made up of any bundle whereof one stick is a broken conscience. So that no social advantage can ever override one man's sacred integrity. Private wrong can never be an ingredient of public right. Privileges may be waived; conveniences sacrificed. This hurts nobody; it is the glory of heroic hearts; and society cannot live richly without it. But duties are inalienable and inviolable. Society, like all God's workmanship, exists to preserve and to multiply them.

One writer defines Society as a system of mercantile exchanges, evidently on the same low conceptions of humanity, and the same materialistic maxims of philosophy, that would limit the ends of Government to the protection of property. The fatal flaw of both notions is, that they ignore the whole upper register of human sentiments, mistake comfort for well-being, and degrade the lofty commerce of spirit with spirit into the vulgar bargaining of political selfishness.

What, then, is our definition of Society? It is the co-existence of men, and families of men, on terms of mutual intercourse, for certain common ends, under the Providence of God. Other creatures are gregarious. Mankind, alone, are social. There are herds of cattle, flocks of birds, shoals of fishes; but in none of these, society. If mankind were associated only to eat, sleep, hunt, and secure animal protection, those brute terms would apply. As they forget their destiny, they do degenerate into droves. But, for society, there must be something more than an affinity for living together. The object of the congregating must be the educating, maturing, completing, of a human nature; rational, affectional, immortal. Go back to the beginning. Given,- the planet in a raw state, centuries of time, and man undeveloped or apostatized; required, to make the earth the abode of a civilized, Christian brotherhood. These are the conditions of the problem. Human society is ordained to give it a practical solution.

To elucidate further the doctrine of society, as we are here to consider it, refer to the nomenclature of science, and so disengage it from other things with which it might possibly be confounded. This doctrine of society is distinct from Anthropology: Anthropology deals with man simply in his relation to other parts of the animal kingdom,—as a member of the zoological system,—marks the points of difference between him and the creatures below him; a branch of natural history. It is distinct, too, from Ethnology: Ethnology deals with the races of men, marks their difference from one another, and notices individuals only as belonging to one or another of these races. It is distinct from Ethics: Ethics is the science of duties, the social duties being considered, but not exclusively; besides, we have other things in society to notice here besides its morality. It is distinct from Theology, of course: Theology deals with the nature and methods of God, and thus of the relations of man with the Divine Life above him; while our subject, though immersed altogether in the truths of religion, touches Theology proper only on one of its sides, or one section of its circle. Finally, it is distinct from Political Economy: Political Economy is the science of those laws which regulate the production, distribution, and consumption of the things in men's possession which have an exchangeable value; in the view of Political Economy alone, the great threefold object of social existence would be "security of property, freedom of industry, and moderation in public expenditure." These are actual social interests, essentials of social welfare. But society exists for something beyond its own possessions.

Let us not hesitate, then, to plant our feet firmly, even by definition, on the broad position that Society is a Divine Appointment. The Former who made us, made us to be social. In the original plan of his constitution, man was not meant to live alone. Though it were possible for every individual of the species to reach the perfection of his private nature in a solitary state,—which it is not,—still, the purposes of God, in his creation, would not be answered. Not so many isolated units, but a Social Body, was clearly the thought that lay in the mind of God when he said, "Let us make man in our own image." Association is not an accident befalling man on his way. It is an inherent promise, want, fact, put into his complex organization at the start. The social state is not a circumstance, but a law: not an economy, but a principle.

Accordingly, as we might expect, in a social state forms of human energy and character come to light which never could be found in the separate person. I have said that to know society, we must first know man. Let it be now remembered, however, that by knowing an isolated specimen of man, we do not know all that belongs to the generic idea of man, or man absolute. Put with that first truth this also,—that as we must study society through man, so we must study man through society. Not only his outward institutions, like Seats of Learning, Institutes of Science, Houses of Mercy, Systems of Commerce, which are themselves a positive good to the individual, but inward traits of the soul, appertain to this social provision of his nature. It is enough to name here affection, conscience, self-sacrifice, sympathy, pity, the loftiest attributes of Humanity, most resembling man to his Maker,—of which more is to be said further on. Thus, while each person may be a specimen of the general capacities of the whole, yet in the social union, which is a compound more complex than any mixed by science, new and independent witnesses come forth to declare the glory of God; just as in chemistry, it has been beautifully shown, that while the combining attraction is between particle and particle, there are yet results,—phenomena, colors, uses, and even forces,—in the combination, not found in the several atoms at all. What was latent in the elements becomes apparent in the compound; and what was dormant in the parts, is active in the whole.

II. Secondly, the social body bears the stamp of its Maker on its origin. This has been denied. On both sides, the question has been argued and learnedly reasoned,—by thinkers, however, whose conclusions have been generally much influenced either by their philosophical or political doctrines, instead of being purely evolved from the elements, and determined by the merits, of the case. Indeed, the origin of society has hardly been considered independently of the origin of political institutions.

One theory of society makes it to spring, not from the Divine will, but out of a mutual league between man and man,—purely human in its scope, purely conventional in its principles, purely accidental in its ultimate destination,—God dethroned from its control, and all Divine signatures swept away from its face. Of this theory the ablest advocate is Thomas Hobbes,* "the philosopher of Malmesbury," born 1588, and writing chiefly about the middle of the seventeenth century. By his system, man finds himself separate from his kind, existing for his own pleasure, "a solitary, selfish animal." As soon as he meets his fellow-man, there springs up a conflict of interests; and, as interest is the only object, they fight. Hostility is the first impulse,—repulsion without attraction. Universal and incessant war is the state of nature. This notion Hobbes supports by such sophistical assertions as that men everywhere arm themselves when they take journeys,—which they do not; that they lock their chests and bolt their doors at night,—which they do, only not against the community generally, but against a few thieves and burglars whom Law has not yet succeeded in overtaking and getting arrested. This fighting savage, however, says Hobbes, finds the universal combat inconvenient and unprofitable. He must eat when he is hungry, and so prepare his food; rest when he is tired, and so prepare his shelter. Industry

* "Leviathan; or the Matter, Form and Power of a Commonwealth." See also Encyclopedia Britannica, Preliminary Dissertation I., by Dugald Stewart; Cousin's critique in his *Cours de la Histoire de la Philosophie;* and Jouffroy's "Ethics."

and comfort require a suspension of strife. All parties bethink themselves of a mutual agreement to let each other alone, and respect each other's property, so far and so long as self-interest prescribes. Hence the restraints and bonds of social and political being. The next step is to guard against new confusions by committing the supreme authority to a single head. An absolute sovereignty, with indefeasible powers, is the result; for any disturbance of these would throw back the whole Body into the primitive discord. The will of the ruler is the standard of right and wrong. Despotism for the State, Atheism for the Soul, Slavery for the People;—legitimate results of a system that starts with making a godless selfishness the fundamental motive of Social Union. Personal traits often throw light on intellectual conclusions. Hobbes was constitutionally a victim of fear, frightened all his life;—the spirit of terror, he says, born with him.* And his biographer says, as he lay dying, he remarked to an attendant, "I shall be glad to find a hole to creep out of the world at." To be sure, his theory of the world was constructed as if it were a place to be crept out of.

Rousseau, whose erratic genius was doubtless one of the efficient causes of the French Revolution

* "Meque metumque simul," are his words.

and of modern individualism, a writer more penetrating than comprehensive, and more brilliant than profound, starts with much the same ideas as Hobbes, but carries them out to totally opposite consequences. With him, too, orderly society, though nominally required by the pure reason, is little else than the result of compromises of self-interest. In his treatise* on the social compact, abounding both in agitating truths, and specious fallacies, he maintains that man voluntarily lays down his natural liberty, or throws it into the common stock, to avail himself of the protection, and more permanent freedom, of a Social Body. But with him, as not with Hobbes, the Body Politic must be a Democracy. There is no sovereign but the people. In all his theory, and with a heart by no means barren of generous impulses, he misses that inwrought law of a disinterested social action and joy, which, a divine germ, planted by God, has been perverted and depraved, but never annihilated. He forgets the Heavenly Thought, out of which all communities really grow. And, by his strange and unhappy misconceptions of Christianity, partly attrib-

* *Du Contrat Social*, 1762. See also his "Discourse upon the Origin and Foundation of the Inequality among Mankind," London, 1761.

For the argument in which Hume combats the theory of Locke, see his essay on "The Original Contract."

utable, no doubt, to a Church that misrepresented it, he lost the very key to a complete social order.

On the other hand, it is maintained, as by Hugo Grotius, the Dutch contemporary of Hobbes, a statesman and a jurist, that though government is strictly human in its origin, it is sanctioned by Providence;* that there are principles of social justice, which would be binding on men living together in a state of nature, even though there were no organized government to enforce them; that neither for the ideas nor the obligations of right does man depend on positive institutions; but, on the contrary, that there is a "natural law, coeval with the human constitution, from which positive institutions derive all their force." Seventeen centuries before, the great Roman Orator and Philosopher, Cicero, had announced essentially the same doctrine in that noble passage: "Right reason is itself a law; congenial to the feelings of nature; diffused among all men; uniform; eternal; calling us imperiously to our duty. Nor does it speak one language at Rome and another at Athens, varying from place to place, or time to time; but it addresses itself to all nations and to all ages, deriving its authority from the Common Sovereign of the Universe and carrying home its sanctions to every breast."†

* *De Jure Belli ac Pacis*, lib. i., cap. iv. † Vid. Frag. De Repub., lib. iii.

Montesquieu, the great Frenchman, sometimes called, by a superb exaggeration, the Legislator of the Human Family, grasps the subject with a stronger hand, and brings to it a richer amplitude of learning. He refutes the theory of Hobbes logically, proving that the passion of *fear*, instead of causing society, presupposes the existence of society. With a much truer insight than his opponents, he makes the desire of living in society the fourth of the original laws of nature,—the other three being the desire of peace, the desire of nourishment, and the mutual inclination of the sexes.*

Coleridge† repeats the refutation of Montesquieu, and adds to it the very important principle, that "fear, in itself, is utterly incapable of producing any regular, continuous, and calculable effect, even on an individual," still less in organizing a community. He ascribes all social order to "the spirit of law," as a natural, inborn, constraining power.

Now, if the object of the present argument were to show the reasons for believing in the existence of God, it would be pertinent to investigate these theories, with reference to the indications actually given, in the social state, that it sprang from the mind of a designer. Assuming, as we do, the fact of a Creator, and only seeking marks of his presence

* *L'Esprit des Lois.*

† In "The Friend."

and character in this particular sphere,—society,—the facts which these theories generally agree in recognizing are sufficient for our purpose. For, they all go to show, that the moment men began to be, they began to be social; that in their social combinations they found utility, welfare, happiness; and that, by the very uniformity of the attraction which draws them together, they are under a common principle of beneficence. Every Philosophy has to assent to the scriptural declaration, that it was "not good for man to be alone." Even the paradox of Rousseau, that a natural state is better than a civilized, will not contradict this; for it is in a natural *society*, not a natural *solitude*, that he finds his Arcadian bliss and his golden age. In the very initiation, the origin, of society, therefore, we see those signs of a Power, and Wisdom, and Goodness Divine, which afterwards unroll and expand into broader and brighter demonstrations.

This, however, we cannot fail to notice, in passing; that, so far from all the conveniences of society existing by the express stipulation of human beings themselves, another law starts into action at the very outset,—viz., that even when men are promoting their own interests, pursuing their own plans, bargaining for their own safety and aggrandizement, all the while they are unconsciously serving each other's weal. Each promotes inevitably the good of his neighbor. The first step in search of protection inures to the benefit of the whole. In the rudest primitive condition, man does not move towards his fellow, without a benignant voice saying from heaven,—through him,—"Let no man seek his own, but every man his neighbor's wealth. For no man liveth to himself."

III. Thirdly, let us advance from the origin of society to its development, watching at each step for the impress of the Maker.

Properly, this branch of the subject reaches back not only to the first appearance of mankind on the planet, but beyond that, to the preparation of the globe itself, through vast cycles of time, to be the theatre of that development. From that hour when the earth, cradled in space, swung shapeless and rayless in its swaddling-bands of vapor, it was making ready for the family that now range its continents, and conquer its wildernesses, and sail its seas, and put a girdle about its circumference, and rejoice in its fruits. Modern geology has left this no longer the guess of a fanciful hypothesis; it is the splendid demonstration of science. Through all the successive formations that have slowly built up and fashioned the outer rind of the sphere,—primary, secondary, tertiary,—plutonic, stratified, and alluvial,—from Silurian to Pleistocene,—not only was the process steady and progressive in the inanimate world towards just that state wherein the race of men could subsist, but by a marvellous correspondence, and through direct successive acts of the Almighty's creative will, the several divisions of animals in their advancing, exhibit a corresponding uniform ascent and approach to the physical appearance of man,—invertebrates, fishes, reptiles, birds, mammals, man. The most deep-sighted students of nature to-day will tell you, and prove to you, that in that inconceivably distant past, when God created the first zoophyte, man was distinctly in his thought. Cuvier, the most philosophic of naturalists up to his day, had just completed his theoretic arrangement of what the exact scale of a complete animal kingdom, in the order of creation, *should* be; scarcely was it finished, when, by a coincidence unmatched in wonder and beauty, perhaps, by anything in the realms of discovery, geology came, took up the solid volume of the rocks, turned over its stony leaves, and spelling out patiently the fossil characters, read off in the order of time, zone by zone, page by page, the confirmation of the great zoologist's conclusion.* "Finally, last born of creation, man appears upon the

* Save at "two special points," explained by Hugh Miller.

scene, in his several races and varieties; the sublime arch of animal being at length receives its key-stone; and the finished work stands up complete from foundation to pinnacle, at once an admirably adjusted occupant of space, and a wondrous monument of Divine classification as it exists in time."

> "From harmony, from heavenly harmony,
> This universal frame began;
> From harmony to harmony,
> Through all the compass of the notes it ran
> The diapason closing full in man."

And not only is the pre-Adamite creation thus prophetic of the individual man,—all the old types of life met and fulfilled in him; not only is the single human brain so "built up as to assume, in turn, the form of the brain of a fish, reptile, bird, mammiferous quadruped, till it takes the unique character of a brain that is human;" not only, as Oken said, is the unit, man, thus "the sum total of all the animals;" but of *man social*, also, a similar prediction is likewise shadowed forth. For, as Coleridge so beautifully asks, "Who that watched their ways with an understanding heart could contemplate the filial and loyal bee, the home-building, wedded, and divorceless swallow, and above all the manifoldly intelligent ant tribes, with their commonwealths aud confederacies, their warriors and miners, the husband folk that fold in their tiny flocks on the honey leaf, and the virgin sister with the holy instincts of maternal love detached and in self-less purity, and not say in himself, behold the shadow of approaching humanity, the sun rising from behind in the kindling morn of creation?"

So it appears, when interpreters of sufficient insight have come to decipher them, that from the very dawn of time, harbingers of human society inhabited the scene of its manifestations; that the race itself, no less than the supreme fact of all its history, the Redemption, began outwardly to be set in order then, in the very frame of things; and that the inarticulate signs of nature echo the supernatural Word, in preparing the way of the "Lamb that is slain *from the foundation of the world.*"

Pass next to the physical materials of this same scene of social development, and see how, at the hour of its beginning, these all afforded facilities for the experiment. Social man, for instance, would want shelter; and the wood and the stone and the other architectural conditions were there. He wanted implements; and Tubal Cain, smiter of brass and iron, found metals and ores for his use, and Jubal became "the father of all such as handle the harp and pipe," — instruments of social festivity. He wanted clothing, and found fleeces, skins, and the materials of vegetable fabrics. He wanted to transport his chattels from one settlement to another, and beasts of burden knelt to take their load, and followed his call. His wandering flocks made him a nomad; he wanted temporary dwellings that he could strike and bear forward; and the hides of beasts and platted and woven textures were his tents. The whole material structure God had arranged into facilities for giving, not the hermit a cave, not the recluse a cell, not the anchorite a den,—but society a home.

Or, turn to the diversities of the surface of the globe; its varieties of territorial form, inequalities of elevation, of climate, of productions, intermixture of water and land. "The Empire of Climate," says Montesquieu, "is the first, the most powerful of all empires." What plan has the Creator written there, for society? Is it not a clear design of social stimulus and energy, of dispersion modified by local attachment, of constant migration and colonization balanced by the tenacity of domestic habit,—the very state most favorable to the swiftest and widest social development? "The continents are made for human societies, as the body is made for the soul."*

* Professor Guyot.

Take the earliest age for an example. As the Patriarchal families, urged by necessity, swarmed and spread, they would strike, even in the same continent, upon new resources in the soil, new provocatives to enterprise, new pursuits for wealth, new motives to industrial competition. As a recent writer* suggests, "If the physical geography of Western Asia resembled then what we know it to be now, almost every remove of the tribes would exhibit fresh variety." Inland exchanges would spring up. Healthy adventures would harden the muscle, and expand the mind, and enrich the blood. "The corn and timber of the terrace-regions would be bartered for the products of the 'land of Havilah, where there is gold, and bdellium, and the onyx stone;' the delicious fruits and fragrant balms of the lowlands for the rock-salt of Anatolia; and horses from the house of Togarmah† for the herds fed on the table lands of Iran." The twenty-seventh chapter of Ezekiel's prophecy is a graphic inventory of this oriental traffic as it had extended in his day.

In later centuries, on broader regions, the same geographic education of society went on. Providence was still the Teacher. On the uplands north-

* Harris in "Patriarchy."

† Ezekiel's name for Armenia.

ward, the hunter chased his game. From the plains of Scythia, suited to pastoral emigration, the roving pilgrims traversed the districts of the East, and defiled through the isthmus of Suez. The alluvial bottoms of the Nile installed a permanent agriculture. Then, as the expanding enterprise of society required it, the Mediterranean offered its tranquil bosom as a highway to the explorer and the merchant.

Indeed, perhaps no single instance of a geographic adaptation is more striking, than that the nascent skill and power of the Human Race should have struck, just as they did, on that water of magnificent memories, witness of the solemn fate of empires, reflecting in its placid face the loveliest scenery of nature and the proudest monuments of art, washing twenty-five hundred miles of classic coast, bewailing with its storms such tragedies of nations and courts! Admitting its tideless waves by the pillars of Hercules, for a rude and timorous, yet persistent, navigation, it exchanged camels for fleets, ships of the desert for ships of the sea, till, in the days of Aristotle, no less than two hundred and fifty maritime cities dotted its shores. Acting itself by the same twofold law that evermore governs the true growth of communities, like the centripetal and centrifugal forces in nature, it at once scattered* men

* "Oceano dissociabili."—*Hor.*, b. i., c. 3.

abroad, and bound them together;—scattered them by its facilities of travel; bound them by its facilities of trade. Then, as they pushed away from the sea, rivers dispersed them along their winding channels; hills proved and quickened their hardihood; forests invited and disciplined their strength. A formidable rampart of European mountains kept the brave sons of the North in their German woods till Providence had ripened the time for their rough wedlock with the softer sinews of the South. An ocean held America in reserve till the old world needed the new and commerce was equal to the Atlantic. Throughout, the features of the earth served the social tuition of men. And every moral peculiarity thus developed, here or there, by visible nature, would gradually modify, through mutual intercourse, all the members of the social family.*

Furthermore, and still keeping your place in the material or physical world rather than the interior or world of ideas, but yet coming in closer and

* See Niebuhr's Lectures on "Ancient Ethnography and Geography."

"Undoubtedly, the relation of man and nature is not a relation of effect to cause, but man and nature are the great effects which, coming from the same cause, bear the same characters; so that the earth and he who inhabits it, man and nature, are in perfect harmony."—Cousin's *History of Philosophy*, sect. viii., second series.

Napoleon deduced the whole history of Italy from the Italian territory.

closer to that, read the design of our social education and development in the Human Body. What geography is to the spirit of history, this corporeal organization, this fleshly microcosm, is to the spirit of individual man. It is the link of a visible connection between the individual soul and the external world, between the personal solitude and the great universe abroad. Notice, then, how admirably the body is contrived for a medium of social communication, a vehicle of commerce in thoughts and feelings, between man and man. Indeed, to such a degree is this destination written out on our frame, that, but for the relationships and interchanges of society, we could not guess why it is fashioned and furnished as it is. To a large extent, it would be a machine without a purpose, a watch without a spring, an engine without the fire, an exquisite electric apparatus without the glowing current that runs and leaps and sparkles in its appointed lines. Examine, in detail, its conformation, its whole, its parts, its limbs and motor-forces, its nerves and senses, its fibre and functions, its sensitive receptiveness, its quickness to all impression, its beautiful balance of passive and active capabilities, its forth-putting energy, its power of positive achievement, and see how expressly it is designed for both giving and taking, in a reciprocal, social existence. Its hands are the pliant, flexile agents whereby, in ten thousand graceful, noble, helpful offices, heart and will in one man minister to heart and will in another, — factors, scribes, executors, porters, artizans;—their friendly grasp, at meeting, the very symbol and firm pledge how each is bound to each. Its feet are the obedient servants and steady carriers by which kindred, neighbors, pilgrims, maintain their mutual connections, sped by friendship, made nimble by charity. Its eyes are not only informers and mirrors for the heads they shine in; they are the subtle and swift conveyers and publishers of every varying light and shade of passion,—their silent, unconscious, but effectual declarations revealing many a sad or mirthful, awful or glorious secret,—pleading, kindling, chilling, tempting, subduing, inspiring. Nay, that throbbing central muscle, the heart itself,—that which is the essential, vital organ of each individual economy,—does not the common figure of language make it the special seat and organ of those affections which join individuals to one another, and thus, not an organ only, but the one great organizer of the world?

Select from among the corporeal faculties only two, for a more complete illustration of the social significance interwoven in the body;—the expression of the human face, and the articulation of speech.

More than we are apt to remember, the human face implies society, because it is so facile and efficient as a means of inter-communication. It is a proclamation of sentiments, which the shrewdest and ablest facial dissimulators can never wholly manage. Napoleon, having much to keep back from other men, and knowing the danger of betraying his emotions, drilled his features as systematically as his battalions, and they tell us of his power of instantaneously discharging his countenance of all expression. But this diplomacy of the face sometimes failed him as disastrously as the tactics of his troops at Waterloo. With all people, the countenance is a basis of confidence or suspicion, love or hate, approach or reserve. If we were made for Robinson Crusoes, every man to his solitary island, the face would not have been made as it is. It is the exhibition-room of the emotions. It is the parade-ground of the mind's styles and uniforms. It is the unguarded rendezvous of all the bodiless couriers of brain and breast. Or, as has been said, "The countenance is the painted stage and natural robing-room of the soul. It is no single dress, but wardrobes of costumes innumerable. Our seven ages have their liveries there, of every dye and cut, from the cradle to the bier; ruddy cheeks, merry dimples, and plump stuffing for youth; line and furrow for many-thoughted age; carnation for the bridal morning, and heavenlier paleness for the new-found mother. All the legions of desires and hopes have badges there at hand. It is the loom where the inner man weaves, on the instant, the garment of his mood, to dissolve again into current life when the hour is past. There it is that love puts on its celestial rosy red; there lovely shame blushes and mean shame looks earthy; there hatred contracts its wicked white; there jealousy picks from its own drawer its bodice of settled green; there anger clothes itself in black, and despair in the grayness of the dead; there hypocrisy plunders the rest, and takes all their dresses by turns; sorrow and penitence, too, have sackcloth there; and genius and inspiration, in immortal hours, encinctured there with the unsought halo, stand forth in the supremacy of light."*

The other great corporeal evidence that man is made for society, as well as society for him, is found in language, and especially language as uttered through the voice. It is a striking symbol of the socially reconciling character of our religion, that it was inaugurated by a Gift of Tongues.† If the si-

* James Garth Wilkinson.

† "Pœna linguarum dispersit homines, donum linguarum dispersos in unum populum collegit."—Grotius.

lent face is expressive, much more is that one specific organ of expression, speech. The first articulate sound the infant breathes is a prophecy of society, a promise of his own development into social forms of life. In that complex and intricate little trumpet, the human larynx, so delicately wrought, so majestic in the compass and variations of its resonance, with its minute ligaments and cartileges, its fine muscles and soft secretions, God has seated a token that man was not intended for a hermit,—whether you regard the faint and early cry by which the listening mother knows and rejoices that her child is not born dumb, or the seraphic melody when the Swedish singer and saint, blending the words of immortal faith with the music of

"The lark at heaven's gate singing,"

enchants two hemispheres, and gives new reality, in every believing breast, to the everlasting assurance, "I know that my Redeemer liveth." For, as another has eloquently asked and answered,* "How does the unseen and spiritual nature act upon surrounding fellow-men, on kindred minds? It manifests itself, it enters into communion with kindred mind, chiefly by the agency of articulate speech; by the twofold interchangeable mystery of intelligible signs—the

* Edward Everett.

one a few black marks addressed to the eye, the other delicate vocal undulations of the elastic air addressed to the ear. To give the spoken word duration, I translate it into written character;—to give the written sign a vital emphasis, I translate it into vocal speech. By one divine art, the dead letter, charged with a living meaning, sounds through echoing halls, and wins or storms its way to sympathetic hearts; by another, the fleeting wavelets of the air are crystallized into a most marvellous permanence, and become imperishable gems of thought, whose lustre no lapse of time can obscure; while, by the union of both, this incomprehensible being, the mind, gently wooed from the vestal chambers of our inmost nature, comes forth like a bride adorned for her lordly spouse, the word; clad in the rich vesture of conversation, of argument, of eloquence, of poetry, of song; to walk with him the busy or secluded paths of life; to instruct and delight the living generations:—ethereal essences as they are, to outlive columns of brass and pyramids of granite, and to descend, in eternal youth, the unending highways of the ages."

I have spoken of the Divine preparation of the world for the development upon it of man's social propensities,—of its geographical distributions as the scene of that development,—of the human body, as having, notwithstanding it is the peculiar property and dwelling place of the individual, marvellous adaptations to the same end. To enter, here, into the signal proofs of this purpose of God, as displayed in the constitution of the interior nature,—the intellect and the heart,—would be to anticipate topics distinctly awaiting us at future occasions. Let us glance briefly, however, at the traces of this appointment discoverable in the obvious aspects and forms under which the social spirit has been embodied.

The great whole that we call Society has been arranged, by the Creator, in a system of concentric circles. The first and smallest social type is the Family. Its primary constituents are a man and a woman,—then parents and children,—sometimes including, in a complete patriarchate, all the descendants of the same living progenitor. The second and next larger is the Tribe, a group of families. The third is the State, varying greatly in extent, sometimes comprised in a single city, like the State of Athens, which, with all its splendor, power and fame, contained only four hundred thousand inhabitants, about two-thirds as many as the city of New York; like the modern Italian republics, Venice, Florence, Genoa; but sometimes also embracing vast territories and populations. Fourth is the Nation, a larger collection, determined by a common origin, a common language, and contiguous lands, often including several political organizations; as Athens, Sparta, Thebes, were all included in the Greek or Hellenic nation. Fifth, and last, is the Empire, a mightier power, a cluster of nations, a ganglion of cities and provinces, and, as the case may be, a heterogeneous combination of different races even, under one civil sway, but growing out of no one principle of life: artificially grappled together by military conquest, by personal ambition, by the intermarriage of royal families, rarely keeping their bulky and unwieldy proportions very long, but stretching out till they break asunder by their own weight:—as the Assyrian, the Roman, the Russian, the British, Empires.

At the centre of any or all of these widening circles stands an individual man, having his social nature, waiting for alliance with his kind; responsible, affectional, but fragmentary and unfinished till he finds his fellows,—holding his place there directly from God above him, as each member of the solar system holds from the sun and yet balances the rest of the members. It is not a single solar system, but many,—the whole also heliocentric,—God the central and supreme Sun of all, not only an attracting Law, not only an irradiating Light, but a conscious Spirit of Life and a Personal Protector.

Towards each of these groups he has a character and a name,—Father of the *families* of the earth, Leader of the *tribes*, Lord of the *states*, King of the *nations*, Sovereign of the *empires*.

Each of these social types has its own political style, or form of government,—the patriarchy, the chieftainship; the democratic, aristocratic, royal, imperial. But society itself is, in a sense, independent of all these forms. It went before their beginnings. It survives their revolutions. It sees them dashed to pieces, and tossed together, reconstructed, or buried, and yet itself lives on, for God is with it, and has uses for it. Its polities may change, and wither; but by principles God has wrought into its being, its own steady growth goes on.

Throughout all the departments of knowledge, in our day, a careful attention cannot fail to discover a universal tendency to generalization and unity—to bring the various operations of matter and of mind under a few grand and simple laws,—to detect the working of identical principles of growth or formation, of development and action, in all kingdoms and provinces of nature. Where before seemed disconnected phenomena, scholars now find interior relations and correspondences,—ever discovering new species, but ever reducing also the number of primal forces.

Where before was confusion, there is order. Where before was complication, there is simplicity. Where before was utter diversity, there is unity. So that the question even arises, whether there may not be reached, at last, one sublime and all-comprehending unity, connecting all sciences themselves by some single law, and in a concord of philosophy and faith, making them all one, even as all must be one in the mind of God. Very certainly, this holds good of that part of the great creation now before us. Society is one fact, springing from one purpose, having one mighty, common life at its heart. Glance over all its divisions and differences, of race, tradition, custom, dress, tongue, color, culture. No matter how unlike the phases, no matter how many the functions, no matter how various the conditions. Underneath all these is one great Social Law and Life, subsisting in the Father's Spirit. We are told, in Natural History, of whole forests springing from a single root. Humanity itself is such a manifold growth in affiliated parts. The old Northmen's fable of the universal Tree whose divine sap is the creative energy, was not so far from the true cosmogony, or doctrine of creation, as those baptized creeds which locate their Deity afar from his creatures in space, or before the Flood in time. The throbbing hearts that warm the world are only pulses from one central Heart of Everlasting, Infinite Love. And whether modern students should conclude that the scriptural ethnology is literal, or only representative,—that all mankind are the descendants of a single pair in Eden, or that the Sacred Record of the earlier age only traces one of several local groups planted by the one God in different climates of the globe, still it would remain profoundly true, that "He hath made of ONE BLOOD all the nations of the earth."

LECTURE II.

SOCIETY A LIVING INSTRUMENT OF DIVINE THOUGHT.

Let us keep distinctly before us the main outline of the argument. 1. To prove that anything manifests the character of the Christian's God, we have to prove that, by the free working of its own nature, it tends to good,—good as we apprehend good by the threefold method of insight, revelation, and experience or history. 2. In the sphere of human life, the first good is character,—character in its best developement as respects quality, quantity, and symmetry; or, to take a classification that squares more exactly with the terms of our general subject, and yet answers to the others, term for term, as respects *man's* goodness, power and wisdom. The proposition will then stand thus:—If Human Society tends, on the whole, to unfold and multiply goodness, power, and wisdom in man, who is God's creature, then it may be held a Divine Workmanship. Its structure, relations, functions, are so many manifestations of power, and wisdom, and goodness in God, the Creator. The first step toward such a demonstration will be, as was attempted in the preceding lecture, to show that in its purpose, its preparation and growth, and its principal normal forms, Society exhibits traces of a plan, on such a scale of magnificence and compass, that no mind, short of the Almighty's, could conceive and execute it.

The next step will be to represent the social state as a practical embodiment, in active operation, of certain ideas which, from all that we know of God, from any source, may fairly be pronounced ideas of God. One leading principle, the same that reigns throughout all the departments of animated nature known to science thus far, must be carefully noted as pervading the whole process,—and we may call it the first of these Divine ideas; this, viz., that with the progress, or elevation of the species is ever associated a twofold result;—an increased variety of individual organization, with a more visible unity of the whole. In other words, Society tends constantly to produce a higher order of men and women, exhibiting a larger variety of persons, yet balanced and reconciled in a more perfect mutual harmony.

It may be asked, however, just here, When you claim that Society is a scene of Divine disclosures and forces, what kind of society do you mean?

It is a compound of many sorts. Do you mean savage society, or civilized,—the Bushmen of South Africa, or the polite circles of London,—the frontier or the capital,—pastoral tribes or centralizing cities? And especially, do you mean a society of Pagans, or a society whose civilization is built on the Faith, and walks in the light, of the Gospel of Christ?

The reply is, we consider Society as to *all* its capacities and powers, including the highest and best. By all means, we must include, in our conception, those forms and conditions of its developement which appertain to its foremost advancements thus far. Because these belong to the true social type. It would be both an irreverent and an unscientific treatment of the theme, to confine ourselves to the lowest specimens. When the naturalist would investigate the turtle, he does not stop with dissecting the coarsest kinds,—the marine varieties of turtle, the loggerhead or the leatherback. Every class must be regarded as embracing its finest known individual. When philosophy contemplates *man,* it does not mean the wild man of the woods, the troglodyte, the barbarian; it does not mean the stupid Asiatic *majority;* it does not mean Caspar Hauser, nor the Aztec children; but man in his best circumstances hitherto — where all his powers have the freest play, his faculties their normal exercise, and where he has shown the best that is in him: simply because all the parts are necessary to the whole,—which whole is, in this case, the realized idea of humanity. When we speak of Rome, even if we credit the fable, we do not mean a wolf and a pair of twins, but what Rome became in the days of Augustus. By New York, we do not understand a Dutch settlement of a dozen cabins, but the New York that has in it a University, Wall Street, Trinity Church, the Cooper Institute; and not only the Five Points, but the Five Points Mission too. If we say the *American* People, we must take in not only the bloody and bruised bodies of prize-fighters, and the brutalized rabble that with equal barbarity look on to see these lumps of muscle battered and borne off on beds from a scene which might have been imported from the playgrounds of the infernals, but we must go up also to the extreme of our generation nearer heaven; we must include our saints, and heroes, and sages,—our Judson, and Tuckerman, and Dorothy Dix,—our Kane, and Herndon, and Tyng,—our Bowditch, and Prescott, and Jay.

And so to analyze and exhibit Society as a fruit of God's designs, our argument does not merely go back to the men and women of caves and dens, dressed in untanned skins of beasts, and eating with their fingers, but embraces the best culture and achievements of both hemispheres.

Again, and as a part of the same query, it is asked, Do we not here attribute to Society, in its own peculiar and self-contained elements, qualities which it derives from a source beyond itself, viz., from religion? Are we not fallaciously finding in a human institution, and as its own natural property, what it possesses only by virtue of the gifts of Christian Revelation?

I answer, Human Society is no less an illustration of God's character and purposes, and therefore no less legitimate and logical for my uses here, because God himself has seen fit to inspire and enlighten it with his own Spirit, through his own Messiah. I say again, Society is presented as it is, in its best manifestations, with all the influences acting upon it, with all the educating forces and ennobling ideas planted in it. Of these educating forces and ennobling ideas we may regard Christianity as one, and the chief. Christianity is capable of being considered either as a disclosure and communication of God, or as a formative power in man. In the latter character, a Religion is just as necessary to any proper conception of man's social state, as intelligence, or natural affection. For man, and social man, is a religious creature. That is, he is created with susceptibilities to religious impression, capacities for religious truths. He is intended for worship and faith. He cannot fulfil his destiny, cannot be the being his Maker designed him to be, without religion. And Christianity is the perfect form of religion,—love of God, and love of man; able, therefore, to produce the highest style of man, *i. e.*, the Christian. It is in this shape only, that it is lawful for my present argument to know Christianity. But to attempt to discuss or examine Society, as a fact, leaving out religion, would be absurd in theory, and impossible in performance. I remark, in addition, that the distinct topic of the relation of Society to Christianity has already been proposed for a future lecture.

Taking a wide observation of social life, not in one spot or community, but in many, not in one epoch, but in the whole historic period, we observe a manifest and preponderating tendency, on the whole, to a more complete and more general realization of the ideas which Society is clearly meant to embody,—such, especially, as a fraternal sentiment between man and man, intellectual activity, a common distribution of the means of life, personal liberty, industry, virtue, religion. Wherever Society is most true to itself, most truly social, its communications and interchanges being most unrestricted and most extensive, there those ideas are most largely unfolded into actions and institutions.

If we find these positions capable of proof by the facts, then we shall be justified in predicating of Society an inwrought law of beneficent activity, just as much as in affirming a law of growth in the tree where the natural conditions of vegetation are supplied, just as much as in affirming a law of assimilation in chemistry where the requisite substances are thrown together.

From the fact that the same social conditions yield similar social effects, we infer, then, that there are such things as *laws of Society*, as there are laws of physiology, mechanics, morals, mathematics; only not so exact, not so definable, not yet classed or co-ordinated by generalizations so comprehensive.* To

* "In the last analysis, history is nothing less than the last counter-stroke of Divine action. Its laws have for their last principle God himself. It is because Providence is in humanity and in history, that humanity and history have their necessary laws. The judgments of history are the judgments of God himself." When Cousin proceeds, from these undeniable maxims, to affirm, in support of his unqualified historical optimism, that every incident in history is in its (providential) place, and arrives for good, he only seems to complicate the problem of moral agency in a sort of Christian fatalism, to ignore the antagonistic quality of sin, and to confound the causative with the corrective Providence. Doubtless, "science suppresses every anomaly," or aims to; but it does not suppress facts. Sin is an enormous fact in history. It is the malignant resistance of the evil in man to the laws as well as *the* Law of God. It is as unscientific as it is irreligious, therefore, to interpret history as altogether justified of Providence.

trace these general principles has been the work of the philosophical historian, in distinction from the mere chronicler, annalist, or recorder. The office of the latter is to report the facts as they occur, discrete and literal, here or there; of the former to combine, to compare, to analyze them, so as to bring out the hidden vinculum that joins effect with cause, and, underneath the shifting, motley play of events that look so much like a dance of accidents, to detect the grand streams of divine thought working sublimely to their destination.* It was some such general principles,

The human phenomena there often contradict the heavenly law, which prevails only by overruling, inflicting terrible penalties on the way.

* It is in the department of philosophical history that the mind of Germany, within the last half century, has rendered, on the whole, its grandest service both to Letters and to Truth. "The religions of the world, the changes of government, the phases of civilization;—the Germans," as has been said, "have not been content to *describe* these, but have searched for *the law* under which they have appeared. The history of mankind has not been handled as a congeries of events, but as an organic developement. Contrast such a history as that of Macaulay (of England) with such a history as that of Neander (of the Church),—both popular examples. The subject-matter of the two works is, to be sure, totally different; but not more so than the methods of the two authors. In Macaulay, you have a glowing description of the progress of events, with brilliant biographical sketches, and the comments of an acute, practical statesman. It is a stage where the curtain rises, and the scenes shift, according to the most consummate art. But when all is over, what deep insight have you gained into the Divine plan of the world? Neander, on the contrary, in his own words, shows us a process having its issue in eternity, but con-

though vaguely apprehended by him, that Aristotle proposed to deduce and make practical for the government of a State. In a more modern time, in the early part of the eighteenth century, Giovanni Vico, a Neapolitan, "a great jurisconsult," and one of the most original thinkers in this department, in a work called "The Principles of a New Science," developed the same view by the method of induction. His doctrine is, that by observing the actual phenomena of social life in many different communities, we may arrive at a definite rule for determining what any given community will be, through the three necessary epochs,—the divine, the heroic, and the human, — and even predict, with accuracy, the length of its existence, and also the date of its decline.* For Vico fell into the unfortunate theory, — since his day generally abandoned,—that the movements of mankind, instead of being on the whole steadily onward, are in a series of circles, or "recurrences," (*ricorsi*,) Society perpetually coming round again, by this cyclical process, to the point from which it started. Throw-

stantly following the same laws, so that in the past we may see the germ of the future, which is coming to meet us."—*Professor G. P. Fisher.*

* Cousin supposes Vico's work to have been "the model and perhaps the source" of Montesquieu's *L'Esprit des Lois.*

ing out that fallacy, Herder, in his "Ideas towards a Philosophy of History," published in 1774, Montesquieu, and Kant, have written from the same sure belief, — that the conditions of social growth may be systematized, — the latter ably maintaining that all the social movements on the planet are slow preparations for one grand ultimate form of universal social harmony, a kind of organized ecumenical commonwealth, where all the parts shall be related to one another, and a central principle of the organism animate and attract the whole. It may now be regarded as the settled conviction of the wisest heads, that social developements are subject to law. From that point, to the conclusion that this law has its seat in the centre and source of all law, in the bosom of God, is but a single step, —and that step we take in obedience to Christian philosophy. "What are all our histories," well asked Oliver Cromwell, "but God manifesting himself, that he hath shaken, and tumbled down, and trampled under foot whatsoever he hath not planted?"*

The laws of Society, then, are thoughts of God. Here, as through the universe, the design has a Designer. So we rise from the contemplation of a social order to a Divine ordainer; from the aspects of regular sequences to acquaintance with Provi-

* See Chevalier Bunsen's work, still in progress, *Gott in der Geschichte*.

dence; from what is called the philosophy of history to the fact of religion. The Family of men has a Parent. Society becomes related to the Creator; earth to heaven. Even ancient heathenism, in its own dark way, accepted this conclusion. Each Pagan people referred the direction of its fortunes to a Deity. Whom they thus ignorantly worshipped Christianity declares to us. The altar they blindly reared, in the midst of their idolatries, to the "unknown God," has been inscribed with the name of the Father of Christ. The great procession of the ages is seen as the majestic unfolding of the scheme of Him who is without beginning of days, or end.

It may be objected that there is too much uncertainty, in the whole proceeding of social life, to let us speak of laws; that it is a whirlpool of happenings; a carnival of impulses; a dance of chances. But look into the analogies of all business, and you see that in what we call chances themselves there is a calculable regularity; over the wildest jumble of events, where every instance seems out of all relation to the rest, presides the firm, majestic sway of Law. Nothing so precarious, nothing so random and whimsical, as not to be rated. Only find out all the conditions, get the data for a deduction, which certainly exist, and you might anticipate for a given community, how many paupers and criminals there would be, how many parties in a season, how many marriages, how many mobs, and how often some agony such as can come only of the breaking of one heart by another will open early graves, or plunge distracted creatures into the drowning that is both death and grave together. What is apparently more fortuitous, or more likely to defy calculation, than self-destruction? Yet in London the number of suicides for the next year can be prognosticated with such accuracy, that men best acquainted with the subject would not hesitate to risk their property on the assurance that in that vast metropolis, of eighteen hundred thousand souls, they will not number less than two hundred and thirteen, nor more than two hundred and sixty-six. There is very little doubt that they will be about two hundred and forty.* We call the calamities of promiscuous travel accidents; yet in a series of years there is a well-known average of such disasters. Even particular crimes, as has been ascertained by most extensive observations, bear a fixed ratio to certain determinable exigencies. M. Quetelet, the ablest statistician in Europe, declares that not only the number of murders, but

* They went up to their highest mark in 1846, the year of the great pecuniary panic caused by the bursting of railway speculations.

the weapons they will be perpetrated with, can be ascertained in advance. All insurance tables are based on this familiar principle. Only the state of knowledge thus far restrains the assumption of risks in those more volatile and fickle actions of moral life where we are apt to expect nothing but surprises and disconnections. We should say scarcely anything is more capricious than the freaks of memory which lead people to drop into the post office letters with a mistaken superscription or none at all. But it would be an easy matter to predict the average number of undirected or misdirected letters in any city post office for any considerable term of years. Of the female population of a country it is found a certain proportion will go about in men's clothing. The relative proportion of the sexes is exact beyond all expectations that would be raised by the conjectures that are applied in anticipation to the individual specimen.

It is no new phenomenon for fallacious attempts to be made to abuse facts by arraying them against truth. Facts of the character here cited are no more to be made a support for the notions of materialists or fatalists, than are the traces of order and law in the physical creation. The first aspect of a newly discovered law often startles us into an atheistic suspicion; but a riper acquaintance with it deepens the confession of our faith.* It is true, the liberty, the sudden self-determination, and the wild inconsistency of the human mind, do greatly aggravate the difficulty of detecting the laws, when we pass from passive realms of matter into the sphere of social humanity. But when they are actually found, and thoughtfully studied, they afford as clear signs of the living God, and as powerful an aid to devotion, in the latter case as in the former. Nor shall we find in the one, any more than in the other, an occasion to question the presence of a sovereign and gracious Disposer, because we catch glimpses of the occult method and the subtle regularities by which he limits the waywardness, balances the individual caprices, and gives uniformity to the mixed results, of the responsible agents whom he forever controls.

It is an interesting incident in literary history, and an evidence of the practical penetration of a mind chiefly known to the world by its speculative excursions in the transcendental philosophy, but before statistical science had attained its present

* The use or abuse made of this law of average statistics by Mr. Buckle, in his recent "Introduction to a History of Civilization in England," naturally throws some suspicion upon it. But its applications, like those of the principle of free agency, or of cause and effect, or of chemical reactions, are as capable of being reconciled with faith as with "Positivism."

degree of maturity, so long ago as 1784, Emanuel Kant, in an essay entitled "Idea of a Universal History in a Cosmopolitical Point of View," wrote as follows: "Whatever be the metaphysical conception of the will, its phenomena, human actions, are determined, like all other natural events, according to universal laws of nature. It is to be hoped that history, when it contemplates the play of the liberty of the will on a large scale, will discover a regular course in it; so that what seems irregular and capricious in individual cases shall appear, as regards the whole species, as a continually progressive though slow unfolding of its original tendencies. Thus marriages, births, and deaths, as the free will of man has so great an influence on them, seem to be subject to no rule according to which their number can be previously determined by reckoning; and yet the yearly tables of them in great nations evince that they happen just as much according to constant laws of nature as the equally inconstant rains whose happening cannot be determined singly, but which on the whole do not fail to maintain the growth of plants, the flow of rivers, and other dispositions of nature, in a uniform, uninterrupted succession."

I. The first fact in social science is the reciprocal relation between society and the individual:

not now, observe, between one individual and another or a particular number of others, but between each and that aggregate of influences, examples, powers, persons, to which, as if it were a unit, we give the one name, Society. A study of our own interior composition is enough to show us that by living alone man will finally become unfit to live at all, — dwarfing humanity, insulting nature, and practically denying God. The absolute segregation of a single specimen from his kind gradually shortens the scope and altitude of his capacities, and distorts his symmetry. Occasional solitude has an unspeakable moral value. Perhaps the loftiest moods are fed from the fountains that spring in its cool and shaded elevations. "Enter into thy closet, and shut the door." The grandest spirits of the world have girded themselves for their heroic works by seasons of lonely retirement: Moses at the mount, with the awful alternations of thunder and silence; Elijah in the cave of the desert, with the wind, and the fire, and the stillness; David in the sheep-cote and the mountains; Paul, three years in Arabia; Luther in his cell; Alfred in the isle of marshes; Columbus, Mohammed, Washington,—all ordained in solitude. Nay, of the Lord and Head of the Race himself, the brief ministry and the eternal redemption must begin with forty days in the wilderness. But notice that in every one of these cases, the solitude is the preparation, not the life. Its very efficacy is in its solemn baptism for the human labor and sacrifice that come after. Through that holy portal of meditation the saints, the heroes, and the Lord passed straight on into service for man. Just there, every species of monasticism fails fatally. It takes the exceptional and makes it normal. It cuts off the uses which mount and desert and closet were ordained expressly to make ready, and renders the gracious hour of prayer to Heaven an indolent and protracted falsehood against the world. He cannot be the true devotee to God who is infidel to man, nor can he honor the Saviour who denies society. In the morning Christ came down from the mountain to the multitude. Those hermits' caverns that bored the mountains of the East into rocky honey-combs, often became tombs that buried the withered limbs of the Church, not chambers nor oratories that refreshed its energies. The lean jaws of asceticism gnawed out sepulchres for truth, but no living home. Even the social lusts and vices were not escaped; for, in idleness and reverie, the morbid imagination threw its doors wide open to their corrupting images, and they who fled from the mammon of the market-place, were sometimes tormented by fiends more fiendish, and devils more devilish, in the cloister.

It has been said that only men's moral sentiments unite them; that the passions are divisive. But this implies a superficial definition of the word *passions*. The passions are not an army of aliens or border ruffians, encamped on the territory of the soul, to besiege it with eternal and irreconcileable hostility. Human nature admits no absolute contradictions. What we call the passions in a bad sense are the unprincipled excesses, the guilty abuses, of propensities the Creator planted in us for social safety, harmony, and utility. At the Fall, man fell *through* his passions not into them. Anarchy was provoked within him. The truth is, every unperverted faculty in us either terminates in or at least harmonizes with social tendencies. You neither enjoy, nor want, very long, except in connection with others. You must impart or display what you have;—you must search out, and earn, or borrow, or beg, from others, what you desire: social acts.

Now, in the animal economy, physiologists tell us, it is an established principle that the elevation of the type is attended by an increased variety in the specific organs; *i. e.*, the nobler the kind of creature, the more complicated the specific parts, yet all embraced under a greater unity and simplicity of plan. Witness a polyp and man,—the extremes of the animal kingdom. A corresponding rule prevails in the kingdom of Society. The more exactly fitted the members of a community are to fulfil the common ends, and to adorn the commonwealth, the more diversified will be their several private capabilities. That will be the noblest people, not where there is the tamest uniformity, but where there is the most striking variety,—as to gifts, dispositions, occupations. Hence, as Society approaches its perfection, there will be more and more developed that "tendency to individuation" which Mr. Coleridge pronounces the true idea of human life.

So, a thoughtful and comprehensive writer on civilization* makes it consist of two elements, and live on two conditions; viz., the melioration of the social system; and the expansion of the individual mind. "Wherever the *exterior* condition of man becomes enlarged, quickened, and improved, and wherever the *intellectual* nature distinguishes itself by its energy, brilliancy, and grandeur,—wherever these two signs concur, there man proclaims and applauds civilization." Everything, as he goes on to show, supports this remark,—common sense, the

* M. Guizot.

nature of both the elements in question, and history. "What, at the origin of societies, have the founders of religion, the sages, poets, and philosophers, who have labored to regulate and refine the manners of mankind, promised themselves? What, but the melioration of the social condition; the more equitable distribution of the blessings of life? We know that if men were persuaded that the melioration of the social condition would operate against the individual mind, they would almost oppose and cry out against the advancement of Society. On the other hand, when we speak to mankind of improving Society by improving its individual members, we find them willing to believe us. Hence we may affirm that it is the intuitive belief of man that these two elements of civilization are intimately connected, and that they reciprocally produce one another."

Again, it is undoubtedly true, that individual strength, purity, integrity, are all put in peril by an excess, or by a corruption, of social mixtures. And it is because man's lower nature can act through the social spirit, as well as the higher. Among its awful prerogatives, Society has it in its power to make men worse instead of better than they are,—to tempt, to mislead, to seduce, to degrade. There are vices that get an easier access, and take a more desperate hold, by social excitements. So, the dominant temper of a social class, or clique, may tend to repress individual freedom, to cripple personal force, to substitute fashion for conscience and imitation for originality, to tone down every heavenly aspiration, to criticise nature into a conventional, Pharisaic propriety, and to razee every fresh, spontaneous moral energy into a respectable, polished stupidity. People ask then, not what is right, true, beautiful; but, what will our set say? This, however, is not the fault of Society, but an outrage upon it. There, certain low-bred, vulgar instincts have usurped the apparatus of social life, meant to be a free vehicle for sincere feeling, and turned it into a non-conductor. Society is indispensable; these are its prostitutions. Society is the appointed agent of joy; there are its infidelities and sins. Society is meant to quicken men by its demands, to nourish them by its sympathies, to call them out to their several best achievements by its opportunities;—but these are the perversions of its power by souls too small to be expanded or too stiff to be moulded to manliness and womanliness by its plastic spirit. Where it is permitted to do its unobstructed work, there it will always be seen striking and preserving just this beautiful balance between the popular and the personal welfare,—between public combination and individual peculiarity, between the general and the private virtue. There you will see it tempering each of the personal vices with a social grace,—self-love with compassion, avarice with generosity, breaking up a morbid introspection by spreading out the broader scenery of other men's experience, cheering gloom into laughter, brightening despondency into humor, genializing misanthropy into good nature, calling us off from petting and nursing our own whims to relieving distress and helping the neighborhood, goading sloth to enterprise, bracing indecision to action, guiding economy between prodigality and miserliness, training insubordination and arrogance to obedience, pouring into the shrunk veins of prudence the fresh blood of enthusiasm, giving to fidelity a grander field, and lifting cowardice to heroism. All these are the regular, gracious, yet half unconscious education that Society is ever giving to our souls; and they show it to be an august Priesthood to man's personal Humanity. And all this is a Law of Society,—a thought of God.

II. Again, Human Society is a grand theatre for the operation of the principle of moral and spiritual reactions; — another Divine idea. Moral possessions increase by being given away. Accumulation proceeds by distribution. The more we give out, for man's sake, the more we take back. Every affectionate act amplifies the heart, and intensifies its power of loving. Without efforts to bless and convert somebody besides yourself, your own soul's convictions dwindle and its circulations stagnate. Obviously, it is only a social nature that makes this principle possible.

In the realms of physical being we meet no traces of it, or, at best, but hints and approximations. There is reciprocal benefit, in order and beauty.* One thing is set over against another, like the rhymes of song, each in its place and season. Even the material creation protests against injustice, against monopoly, against interference; her every product has its use; every particle its service; every form or fibre its task or its loveliness. But there she stops. Light emanates and is reflected; but neither sun nor star is brighter for shining. Vegetation gives out and takes in, by its generative and respirative processes, but its fine equilibrium is never emancipated into voluntary and at the same time self-fertilizing benevolence. The rose is no sweeter for the fragrance with which it perfumes the morning; nor the stream fuller for its liquid gift, — its "cup of cold water," — to the meadows. Among animals, such dumb and sponta-

* See Lecture IV.

neous attachments as unite tribes and families, the likings of the mother bird and of the more companionable brutes, are bound fast by the old limits of instinct; they rarely rise to the dignity of sympathies, and they nowhere reveal the moral grandeur of growing stronger by a conscious, principled exercise.

The moment we ascend, however, to social man, the tokens of this noble law stand forth in splendor. There light *is* made more lustrous by scattering its beams,—none growing wise so fast as they that teach, every intellectual perception sharpened by imparting knowledge, every will fortified by effort, every heart made better by beneficence. They that *do* the most, *are* the most,—the quantity of being ever multiplied by the uncalculating generosity of its bestowment. That manhood, or womanhood, is the richest, which spends most for some unpaying interest of humanity. Find out that pair of eyes which look abroad with unobtrusive mercy into the domestic distresses of the brotherhood; find out that pair of hands which are ever busy working the thing that is good for some needy or troubled neighbor, and you may be sure they belong to some Good Samaritan or Sister of Charity, who, whether prosperous or unsuccessful as the world judges, is affluent with more than the wealth of "barbaric pearls and gold." Piety itself often gets diseased for want of this energy in communicating itself. Natures that incline more to reverie than to work find their religious progress unsatisfactory. Many believers, sincere enough in their convictions, as sincere as any inactive believer can be, are mischievously hindered in the true progress by the mistake of supposing that Christian duty terminates in self-improvement. Faith is soon but a withered root, unless it bears flowers and fruits. None of us are appointed to walk to heaven alone; and it is doubtful if any of us will ever get there who do not, somehow, help some other soul thither. The best nurture for personal religion, after prayer, is an effort to spiritualize some child, house-mate, acquaintance, or heathen. If you draw back your hand, when it is invited to a beneficent task, the spiritual muscles are gradually paralyzed. If you tightly close the fingers over the mouth of your purse, when there is a fair opening to give something to extend the kingdom of heaven, by a book, a church, or a missionary, then you pinch, at that moment, the dimensions of your own soul. "Give, and it shall be given unto you."

As this is a principle which has its purest activity in the highest, that is, in the spiritual part of man, we must naturally go, for instances and illustrations of it, to the spiritual plane, and the organization that specially represents that part, which is the Church. All the revolutionary movements that have extended the kingdom of Christ, disturbed formality, and dethroned dogmatic error, sweeping across slumbering communities, have been accompanied by intense missionary zeal, either domestic or foreign, by immense and willing sacrifices of money and comfort for the Gospel's sake, by earnest and enthusiastic aggressions on practical unbelief, sensuality, Paganism. Whatever sect presumes to take a place as a member in Christ's body without this activity does not "abide in the Vine," and must expect to be cut off as a dead branch. The Head of all these members has impressed it on the whole organization, that whatsoever limb does not give, to that it shall not be given.

Seek illustrations in the actual history of the Church. Whatever prevailing form Christian faith has taken, activity from the centre outward has been the uniform condition of success, and the invariable sign of life. When the Church has been doing most outside of itself, it has had most vigor within itself. Its periods of self-sacrifice have been its periods of glory. Such is the reactive force of spiritual industry. In the apostolic age, the brightest and most wonderful ecclesiastical era, almost the entire work of the Church was of this sort. The genius of Christianity then, having planted and established a church in any place, could hardly afford to stop to watch over it,—but flew on, from country to country, from island to island, from city to city, eager to kindle new fires in every seat of darkness. Those brave and ardent men not only gave a part,—they gave everything, — houses, property, reputation, comfort, blood, — they gave themselves. Thus, while they gave without stint, "it was given to them without measure." Later, the mediæval church, in the midst of its errors, was strong at home, just in proportion to its zeal abroad. Read the history of Jesuit missions in South America, in Canada, in India, and all the East. When Protestantism came, it was as a missionary cause that it advanced and triumphed. Since that time, there has always been a most significant and providential coincidence between the waking up of religion into practical power, and its endeavors to extend itself to the destitute.*

It is unquestionable that when the spirit of missions broke forth in Protestant England, the religion of England was saved from impending extinction.

* See Examples in "The Great Commission."

There is even reason to believe that had a single heathen never been converted, the impulse given to Christianity at home by the movement, and all its generous influences, would have justified the entire expenditure, because no other expenditure of the same means could have accomplished the result so effectually. The dull monotony of preaching and worship was at once broken up, all over the realm. The slackening bonds of union and sympathy between churches and ministers were forthwith tightened. Mutual suspicions and jealousies were scattered. Discords were healed. The whole religion of the country became practical, pure, and substantial. Under the general invigoration, a cluster of kindred philanthropies sprang into being; for it is the nature of no real beneficence to live alone. We may say what we will of charity beginning at home, the historical fact is found to be that most is done at their own doors, by those who stretch their arms the widest,—for the very palpable reason that a beneficent spirit, when kindled, works in all directions. When we hear the celebrated Andrew Fuller telling of that period in his ministry when he sought by every means to remove the clouds of darkness and doubt that had settled down on his parish, but sought in vain, till suddenly the interest of the new movement for heathendom seized on his people, — and then how the women began to collect money, and the men to take counsel, and all to work and pray, so that before they were aware every complaint ceased, "the sad became cheerful, and the desponding calm," simply because "God blessed them while they tried to be a blessing;" when we learn from the record of the earliest British Baptist missions, how, when the cause became popular, religious indifference gave place to righteous living, backsliders were restored, fears were dispelled, and peace and strength were renewed, — we begin to see how true it may be that even Macedonia, Nestoria, and Labrador, by only lifting up their supplication for help, may become apostles that reconvert a declining Christendom to Christ.

So in particular local bodies. There is no promoter of parish life, or peace, like liberal sacrifices to extend the cause, and build up new parishes. The social law comes in to bind, as well as to build. The church that shuts itself up in its own privileges, contents itself with occupying its own pews on Sunday, lounges on its own cushions, and takes an epicurean satisfaction in its own culture, or choir, or opinions, or architecture, or preacher's reputation and eloquence, is smitten and accursed, in its violation of this law. The contribution-box becomes a kind of spiritual thermometer. If Providence were to resuscitate one of our sleek, well-fed, fashionably dressed, self-righteous congregations, dying of ecclesiastical luxury and rhetorical surfeit, he would turn it out into the lanes and homes of the poor, invigorating its dyspeptic faith by earnest works of charity.

In all the operations of this reactionary power we see one of the most majestic proofs that in the highest interests of man, his social nature plays a leading part, and that this particular action of that nature is a design of God.

III. There are, furthermore, certain great moral ideas of God's own Being, which he has evidently created Society to work out into visible shapes on earth. They reside in his own perfect Life. They are also the Divine glory of Humanity. They form the essence of all we know of Morality. A brief reference to these will serve our immediate purpose. They are Right, Truth, Love, Liberty. We may take these either as principles for man, or as attributes of God. Society is a means God uses to set them forth, and put them into practical power on earth.

1. The first, by its radical importance to the very existence of Society, has always been represented by an actual institution, viz., Government.

Logically, the basis of Government is the need of Justice between man and man. But practically, you say, the actual Government often turns out the foe of justice. Nevertheless the Government is still, and evermore, the struggling, aspiring, and persevering endeavor of the people to realize Right. From the beginning, Society has been working towards that end. Logically, the Ruler should be the justest man of the nation. Practically, he may be a military conqueror, like Nimrod, Tamerlane, Bernadotte, Napoleon I.; — or he may be a petty diplomatist and imitator, like modern Kings and Presidents, too many to mention;—or he may be a cruel and selfish tyrant, like the tyrants of Italy, Spain, and the East; or he may be only the son of his father, like Bourbons and Stuarts. Where the governing power shall at any given time be lodged, is a question of many answers. "In the will of the Prince," say Hobbes, Machiavel, the Austrian Catechism, and despotisms generally. "In the will of the People," say Milton, Locke, Jefferson. "In *some* representation of the wisest part of the People," say the Federal Republicans. But through them all, — and this is the thing of impression and beauty and meaning,—through them all Law is vindicated, stern, kind mother of our peace. The eternal distinction is kept alive. Society repeats its claim for equity. Justice is advanced, — blessed guaranty of every social bond. The powers that be are ordained of God. Right is held up, and borne on, to her slow but patient victory.

"Careless seems the Great Avenger; History's pages but record
One death-grapple in the darkness twixt old systems and the Word;
Truth forever on the Scaffold,—Wrong forever on the Throne,—
Yet that scaffold sways the Future, and, behind the dim Unknown,
Standeth God, within the shadow, keeping watch above his own."

2. So with Truth. Veracity is a social virtue. Society nurtures it, tries it, manifests it. In solitude, it would miss its most generous action, even if we can conceive of its existence. Falsehood may sometimes bear Truth down. Cunning may pervert it, self-interest may stifle it, hypocrisy may betray it. Yet through all that conflict of long ages, and by man's social nature, Truth is steadily rising to her empire, building her eternal throne on the ruins of Error. He reads the Past backwards who does not see in all social clashings and conflicts the inevitable process that is to make man true with man, base institutions on probity, not on cant, superstition, or heresy, and through ten thousand experiments and contests show how God himself is True.

3. As to Love: to say that Love is a social virtue is mere tautology. It has appeared that the force which draws and cements Society,—and makes it to be Society,—cannot be hate, cannot be fear, cannot be sordid self-interest, nor any of the repulsive passions: for the simple reason that, in morals as in physics, repulsions never attract. One principle constructs Society, as one will marshals the stars. If He whose name is Love had been seeking only a scheme to exhibit, in free play, the first attribute of his own nature, Human Society would be the result,—with its mutual dependencies, its parental instincts, its gracious sympathies, its spontaneous charities, its brave and loyal devotedness. These, too, must contend with their opposites. Free will must find antipathy, and jealousy, and revenge, and spite to be possible. The two powers, Light and Darkness, Ormuzd and Ahriman, must fight their battle out. We only utter the general human instinct when we pronounce malice, with its great engine, war,—malice in all its shades, and war in all its shapes,—to be anti-social. But malice dies; the affections are immortal. And ever since the solitude of the unwedded Adam was broken by the coming of his bride, through lapse and recovery, through alienation and redemption, the Race has been feeling its way

forward to the fulfilment of the promise,—"Peace on earth; good will to men."

4. Finally, Freedom. Through what an august succession of national tragedies has God led mankind, that he might teach them the folly and the wrong of oppression,—the glory of that Liberty with which Christ makes his people free! What experiments of sorrow! What lessons of ruin! What baptisms of blood! There you read, again and again, how tyranny is anarchy, how the immortal spirit in chains thirsts insatiably for emancipation, how a man under the heel of his fellow is ever a magazine of terror, how slavery is death. See the conditions of the problem, and then the demonstration. See a fertile, inexhaustible soil, a lovely climate, open markets, stout, able-bodied negroes, just kidnapped, or fed and reared up to sixteen hours' work in the twenty-four, with a present cost of maintenance of only a pint or two of flour and a salt herring a day. What should prevent unbounded accumulations of wealth and every outward advantage to the planter, then? Nothing, perhaps, if man, the animal, were all. But there is a God of Liberty and a God of Sabaoth, in heaven, who has planted his social Family for other ends, into whose ears the cry of the oppressed hath entered, and will enter forever; and so, instead of durable

riches and honor, impoverishment, vice, degradation! On the one side a few proud, opulent, indolent nabobs, whose children wither and corrupt by laziness and sloth; on the other, a beggared, short-lived, terror-struck population, with mortgaged estates of exhausted lands! See, the tyrant and slave-owner is himself but "a slave turned inside out;" even as Gibbon says it was in the Byzantine palace,—where the emperor was the first captive of the ceremonies he had imposed. See an East India Company, by a career of cruel aggression on a country full of the materials of wealth, acquiring a debt of fifty millions sterling, and what besides of retributive carnage and horror, let the daily British journals, and the wail, yet moaning in thousands of British households, tell. See the splendor and majesty of Rome rotted by slavery. See the taxation of American colonists reacting into a Revolution of independence, and taxing the mother country herself for a hundred millions. See everywhere illustrations of the true saying of Lamartine: "Man never yet fastened one end of a chain round the neck of his brother, that God's own hand did not fasten the other end round the neck of the oppressor." See, from first to last, what Napoleon himself had finally to confess, that "without justice there is no power." See, in a word, that over all social communities and ranks, rules a Nemesis whose name is the Lord of Love, Almighty.

"For He that looketh high and wide,
Nor pauses in His plan,
Will take the sun out of the sky,
Ere freedom out of man."

LECTURE III.

SOCIETY A DISCIPLINE OF INDIVIDUAL CHARACTER.

It was attempted, in the two former lectures, after defining Human Society, to show, first, that it is a divine appointment in itself; and secondly, that its Laws and its Principles are the Creator's thoughts and purposes. In order not to anticipate subsequent steps, the argument was there confined, for the most part, to Society as a whole, without a detailed investigation of its particulars. I spoke of the impress of God's design to be seen on its origin, on the scene and the manner of its external development, and in the providential ideas which it represents and tends more and more to embody.

Not that everything in social life is divine. Christian philosophy admits no such loose, perverted optimism as that. Because we discover that God has certain definite intentions in the social constitution, we are not therefore at liberty to infer that the whole operation of Society, and all its temporary or local effects, will be what a God of justice and love approves. The design is one thing; the hindrances, from man's evil, through which the design is worked out, are another thing. The electric fluid does not accomplish its passage by a straight path, but follows the line of least resistance. Account for it by whatever theory we may, depravity must be admitted as a fact consequent upon moral trial. Doubtless the disturbing influences, emanating from the passions of mankind, which now are suffered to mix and confuse the currents of history, might be borne down by Omnipotence ; the sea of human affairs might be swept into a flat monotony by the irresistible wind of an arbitrary will. But *then* the Almighty's government would be another economy from the actual one, nor would he be God.

It is necessary especially to remember this, as we now come to treat of Society as a discipline of individual character. God uses our social relations to exercise us, and ripen us, in the qualities of personal virtue and the strengths of a right life. He sets us down on a social planet, surrounds us with fellow-beings, implicates us in a promiscuous play of passions, that through this intermixture, friction and conflict, each and all might grow into ampler proportions, into stouter fibre, into a more flexible activity. Yet we must not expect to see this result produced with a fatal uniformity. Moral freedom remains. Heaven itself jealously guards forever the sacred liberty of choice. It is like any other opportunity of pupilage. You may learn and grow wise if you will. If you will, you may slight your lesson and be a fool. The social laws act for us, but they will not compel us.

The main proposition is simple, and it is this: In making man what man was meant to be, the Creator first gave him a social nature, and then set him down in social surroundings. How the former is acted on by the latter, the soul by Society, is what we have now to illustrate. In such a review, the resort must be to familiar scenery,—sights and sounds that are seen and heard of all men and women. Here history will not serve us much, because history, as it has been hitherto written, has less to do with the secret life and real experience of humanity than with its public exploits, its policies, dynasties and battles; less with its spirit than its forms; less with men and women, the people, than with their captains and managers. Treatises can here help us little, because, as we have said, social laws are not reduced to a scientific system. The argument must proceed by passing before us some of the principal forms in which Society exists, to discover in them influences which are their own moral evidence, and a spiritual significance which is a manifest demonstration of God.

These will be, chiefly, the seven social types produced by kindred blood, by unequal strength, by the instinct of sympathetic entertainment, by trade, by local habitation, by congregational emotion, and by public opinion.

Approach, then, these permanent and familiar forms of social life, to observe how they are ever carrying forward their educatory work, and vindicating their office as providential schoolmasters.

I. First, and simplest, is the Family. There the sensitiveness of affection, the closeness and constancy of contact, the felt need of mutual trust and boundless tolerance, the immense freight of happiness staked on implicit confidence, render every household a most critical and exacting test of genuine goodness. It is a superficial notion that in the sacred enclosure of domestic habit, all virtue is particularly natural and easy. On the contrary, the very value of the love that ought to reign there, the very beauty of the tenderness that ought to soften all the asperities and adorn all the drudgeries, the very charm that ought to invest the homely routine of task-work, and dignify with fresh enthusiasm the dullness of drooping spirits and weary nerves,—all this only doubles the bitterness of disappointment when the ideal Paradise is lost, or never found. There, as everywhere, in proportion to the sacredness of the place, and the immensity of hope, is the cruelty of the desecration and the torture of sensibility, when the first disappointing discord jars the air. We all know how hard for pride it often is to take the frank fault-finding of housemates, simply because conscience whispers they know us best, and the blame must be real. Each understands the other's weaknesses, and a censure there is like the decree of doom. Besides, it is in the eyes of those we love most that we long to be most approved, and their dreadful discovery of our infirmities is a wrench of pain. The truth is, there is no spot on earth, no Delos of inevitable peace, not even the blessed Eden of our home, where the impulses of kindness can supersede the tuition of experience, or the promptings of nature dispense with the principles of religion.

And therefore God sets our childhood into the Family, as into a solemn, cheerful, difficult school for its faculties. Therefore he has appointed that the human spirit shall first wake to consciousness, feel its first ties, confront its first trials there, under those tones of the mother's voice, which, it has been beautifully said, no skill of vocal art could ever imitate, and amid those expectant, encouraging affections, which tempt out into exercise every nascent energy. Therefore he has ordained marriage, and immured it with care and love and modesty, guarding its pure precincts as much by spiritual attractions as by terrible penalties, rebuking the vulgar frivolity that trifles with its sanctities and degrades its gates by jest and gossip, by levity and license; yes, trifles and degrades, as if the satire that once called wedlock "going home by daylight after courtship's masquerade," and the old Russian marriage formula to the bridegroom, "Here, wolf, take thy lamb," were the highest philosophy of the theme. Therefore he has adjusted, since the first pair, the proportion of the sexes, balancing the local preponderance of the one or the other over against some special waste, and that of the males on the whole against their greater liability to exposure and destruction. Therefore he has accumulated, in kindred blood, from generation to generation, the hereditary seeds of peculiar dispositions, traits, temptations—running the lines of succession down through all the meshes of general diversity, making the Past as well as the Present to shape us. Therefore he has surrounded the dawning life of perception and reason with the marvellous patience of parental care, yet writing on every new-born child the fearful warning against parental folly or neglect. Therefore he has reciprocated the parental and filial offices, making the offspring not seldom a refiner and even rescuer of the father and the mother,—a "little child leading them." Therefore he has blessed brothers with sisters, and sisters with brothers, tempering manliness with gentleness, inspiring the delicate soul with courage, and, by a thousand reciprocities of strength and weakness, of older and younger, of comers in and goers out, joy and grief, decision and amiability, mirth and tears, and daily looks of faces and tones of talk, has organized a curriculum of moral study under domestic roofs, more complicated, and yet more simple, than the oldest university ever saw. The Family is the primary institution of all social order and peace. It is that ordinance which Jehovah wrote in nature, and Christ reaffirmed in words, making one woman the wife of one husband, and their wedlock the bond of every social good.

II. A second method of the discipline of character is afforded by the relation of the employer and the employed. Every one of these relationships, we shall find, however accidental or merely economical it seems, engages a new part of our nature, and exercises a new set of dispositions. What looked like a mere expedient of domestic convenience—as the employment of servants, clerks, porters—the God of our life takes up and makes a portion of his great social plan for maturing our souls. If we watch it in this view, we shall see that in this peculiar intercourse there is exercised a kind of morality less animated by the affections than that which acts in the Family, less guarded by equality of position and the mutual assertion of legal rights, or any other intimidation, than in Society at large. Honesty of dealing, for instance, when the other party to your bargain is your equal in knowledge and position — a shrewd, practised trader, competent to the arts of traffic — implies a different pitch of virtue from honesty with one who is weak, uninstructed, partly overawed and disabled with a sense of social inferiority. Not that there are two kinds of honesty : but the altered conditions test it in different ways and degrees. Then the very fact of partial dependence, obtaining not so much in actual servitude, as in most proletary classes, elicits in the conscientious master or employer a distinct order of sentiments—a considerateness, a feeling of protection, a blending of parental vigilance with magisterial authority—conducive to a peculiar kind of righteousness. By the benignant compensations of a Providence that nowhere leaves the worst badness without its grain of good, it is in this quarter that we find, in some forms of slavery, the ounce of benefit which obstinately holds out against all the tremendous weight and complication of wrong. Vassalage, serfdom itself, in an age when Christianity has not yet created a conscience against it, is a moral opportunity to the lord of the soil. Feudalism, while it limited the despotism of kings by keeping power and arms in the hands of the baron and the noble, on the other hand offered to these a generous culture in honor and compassion. No domineering institution, whatever its abuses, is suffered to break asunder the connection of these divine compensatory rules. You have not learned of your fellow-citizen whether he is a tyrant or a republican, liberal or mean, nay, a Christian or a knave, till you know how he treats the laborers in his field, the operatives in his factory, the clerks in his store,—looking, too, not only at wages or bodily comfort, but at their human feeling, their families, their evenings, their Sundays, their brain and heart. A housewife's character is no more revealed, nor even tried, till you follow her from the assembly and the church to watch her temper, her tones, her manners, with cook and seamstress and nursery-maid, than an actor's private thrift can be inferred from the fine speeches and glittering costumes of the stage. In the one case her virtue was on exhibition, and was performed; in the other it was at home and itself.

III. Come, however, next, as the next wider scene, to a company met for social entertainment. "We receive," says Montesquieu, "three different educations,—of our parents, of our masters, and of the world." Come, then, to that brilliant throng,—an evening party,—that less professional but not always less scenic theatre,—that more promiscuous enlargement of the household,—that gay yet solemn match-ground and Olympian competition of all the passions and principles of men and of women, so festive and yet so tragical,—such bubbles and spangles of air and light dancing on the surface, such plots and counterplots, ambitions and artifices only a little way beneath;—but, oh, sometimes such mortal struggles of despair and peace, of love and fear, of jealousy and candor,—nay, such writhings of immortal demons and angels, far down in the deeper abysses of the unsounded soul beneath!

It is a scene like this, indeed, which, just because it is so lively and expressive a symbol or representative of what we are most apt to understand by social life, has taken and appropriated to itself, in many circles, as by exclusive application, that undefined, uncertain name, Society: so that people flippantly and narrowly say of their neighbors, according as they are or are not seen in such assemblies, that they are, or not, *in society*.

Now, to realize the discipline such a gathering carries on, only consider the actual emotions which there jostle against each other; get nutriment or poison, get elbowed or courted, get sunny favors or chilly neglect or frosty scorn, get the warm hand or the cold shoulder, get smile or sneer, get equal honor or insulting patronage. Is it possible to move on such a spot—call it battle-field or play-ground as you will—to stand among its flatteries, its criticisms, its concealments, its confessions, its conversational tactics, its gymnasium of ready and nimble thoughts, its phantasmagoria of complimentary nothings and dreary emptiness, its supple turnings of expression, its sentences begun in frankness but cunningly shaped, before they are finished, by some prudent recollection—is it possible to stand here, and then go out from a tuition like this, without being better or worse? Many a young girl, that lays off her ornaments after her first party, weary of the polished insult that has offered her only a frivolous flattery, as if her womanly soul could be content with that, or else giddy with the first tones of the silver-tongued sorcerers, has taken on her spirit that night the influence that sways her forever,—making her yet the strong conqueror of herself and minister of light to others, or else the woman of pleasure that is "dead while she liveth," and never to live truly any more. See the strong there bearing the infirmities of the weak; see genuine kindness seeking out the unknown, exploring the corners of the room to entertain the timid, the ugly, or the unsocial; see the self-forgetful devices of the simple desire to please; see the graceful sacrifices, each for each, of the loving and beloved; see true politeness waiving every unwelcome topic, hiding the heart's unsightly spots, and catching, by trained perceptions, the disguised signals of mortification or painful memory, only to ward off the annoying allusion, while petty malice or weak pride pushes the irritated sensibility, and exults in smiting the bruised reed; see ruinous prodigality, and over against it as ruinous a parsimony; see the love of admiration producing its mixed results,—refinements, adornments, amenities, all the way from the savage who tattooes his skin to the last fashionable decoration of his most exquisite civilized cousin; see an honesty of speech valiant as that of martyr ages or soldiers' camps, yet courtly as that of halls of state; see sincerity like that of the little child: I say, whatever else this motley company may be, it is no mark for contempt, simply because human creatures are so wrought and proved there for the Judgment.*

* I have seen, in one of the bright books of the day, a sort of argument coolly constructed against the reasonableness of broken hearts, or rather of letting them ever be broken: and thus a protest against the mutual dependencies of social affection. "Human beings," says this easy author, delightfully disposing of all the deeper tragedies of the

To discover this the more completely, distinguish between this social intercourse as it is apt to be, and as it ought to be,—especially with reference to those two strong pillars of a muscular morality, veracity and courage. True social intercourse is not a formal association of people, moving under artificial prescriptions, yoked by domineering customs, hoodwinked by traditional conventions, "presenting their compliments" on handsome paper, when they have really nothing to present but suspicion or spite,—"very much regretting" they cannot be present where they secretly rejoice with all their hearts not to be,—"requesting the honor and pleasure" of company which they know will be rather a visita-

human heart by a statement shot at the head,—"human beings hang not on one another in that blind way. We have each an individual soul. On another soul may rest all its hopes and joys, but on God only rests its worth, its duties, and its nobility." Hence there is no need, anywhere, in all God's world, of what men mean by a "broken heart!" O fluent and complacent philosopher, I thought; how much deeper lies the truth than this plummet sounded! "On another rest all its hopes and joys," and yet no possibility of breaking! Yes: its worth, its duties, and its nobility do rest on God. And so rests there, blessed be his Pity! the heart, that, just because of the infinite capacity he gave it for love and hope, is broken here,—never to be bound up but in the healing air of heaven. Human beings do hang on one another, not in any blind, but in that fearful, way. And so must they be judged, and comforted,—the breaker and the broken. The awfulness of our natures is the trust they are to each other. The infinite ocean,—joy, misery, affection, despair,—heaves and swings its tide in every breast; but how would it all shrink to a drop, and even that drop dry up, but for the breasts that heave and beat around it!

tion than a visit,—and "renewing the assurance of their distinguished consideration" for persons whom nothing but self-interest keeps them from insulting to their faces, or slandering behind their backs. This is a Society of etiquette, hypocrisy, cowardice, ceremony, and diplomacy, *not* the incarnation of divine ideas. The four preceptors of that training are policy, pretence, imitation, appetite. Nor is it properly *human,* seeing how many of its elements it holds rather in common with the fox, the crocodile, the ape, the peacock, or even with the devil and his angels.

The social company that a divine education contemplates is a far nobler and far holier thing. It is gathered by common sympathies, grouped by real affinities, seeking a liberal and harmonious development of all the best powers of the race. It is, as we saw, the beautiful balance of individual peculiarity with a collective unity,—carefully respecting the liberty of the one while it guards the order of the other,—engaging a salient and racy variety of persons while it binds together the whole diversified *kosmos* by the centralizing gravity of mutual good faith. In a word, it is a Christian Society, rooted in Christian convictions, expanding by a Christian culture, culminating in a Christian commonwealth. The rectitude of the lowest born or bred is of deeper significance than the pleasure of the highest. Divine in its institution, it is human in all its experience, having for its eternal Head that wondrous soul who blends both these elements in the august mystery of his mediation. It is born of God, and inspired by Christ, for the perfecting of mankind. It may exist in its essence wherever the proffers of hospitality, the sacrament of marriage, the emergencies of enterprise, the hopes of learning, the instincts of neighborhood, the faith of the church, gather two or three together. Different lives touch. The germ of it is the Family. The full, unfolded crown and completeness of the growth, the living dome, encompassing flower and fruit and leaf and bough, is the universal Family of the Race. You find it realized partially in schools, in literary clubs, in leagues, in legislatures, in nations. The same marvellous play of acting and reacting influence pervades the sewing-circle and rustic husking-party as the senate or tournament,—the children's summer pic-nic as the royal reception. The same angels of mercy stand waiting with faces half unveiled. The same fiendish envyings, calumnies, revenges, peer and scowl out of the shadows behind:—God's discipline forever.

We have all heard of the little girls that "wished they could have company all the time," and when asked why, said, "Because then father would be always good-natured." There is the revelation of a principle. To be sure you might say, the company made this surly or petulant father a hypocrite. Perhaps not; perhaps the temporary elevation was real, and the self-control sincere; perhaps the company was only a wholesome intervention between him and a contentious, impracticable influence from the other side of the house,—a relief like one of his public conversations to Socrates. But what if it did, in that case, occasion hypocrisy,—the tribute vice pays to virtue? It would only show that the company exacts a higher style of behavior than privacy. The fact is, Society is a kind of judgment. Together, men are more in awe of their own standards of right than alone. There is a shamefacedness about contemptible foibles, and even sins. The law of duty, up to the sense of the average recognition, and generally a little higher, gathers a cumulative force and awfulness. The suppression of overt evil is exemplary. The restraint is a discipline.

I spoke of courage. The social company is a school for that. Fashion is the imperial tyrant, of which local opinion, unjust law, the privileges of currency and popularity with your class, may be only the too willing ministers of state,—adding specific chains and caprices of their own to the ascendant cruelty of their liege. Resistance, by principle, to that, will be a braver valor, very often, than the facing of batteries or bayonets. I spoke of veracity. When shall the prophet come, in camel's hair, and leathern girdle, that shall uncover the abysses of our acted falsehoods, and pour adequate shame on our systematic impostures? Smiles on our faces, with bitterness underneath; cordiality in our grasp, with no nerve between the fingers and the heart; love, marriage, all holy trusts, made merchandise, and auctioneered to the loudest bid; invitations of courtesy bringing the company together by one lie; greetings of indiscriminate and extravagant welcome receiving them with another; composite illusions dressing and decorating them with another; ceremonies of elaborate make-believe, mocking reality with another; and insincere regrets at the farewell dismissing them with another; — who will dare to affirm these do not enter appallingly into what we call elegant life? Or who will venture on the yet bolder and more faithless denial that the final cause of these exposures is to hasten the advent of that rugged, truth-speaking, Christian time, which shall rend apart these guilty impositions, and restore the social world to its upright simplicity?

IV. Reference has been made to commerce. Trade

is essentially a social institution. It is one of the departments in this great unsystematized university of social discipline, whether by its regular processes, or its periodical dislocations, panics and convulsions. I cite, therefore, as another illustration of my subject, that vast and world-encompassing interest, whose laws and fluctuations not only determine the material welfare of men, but strike down also into moral obligation and the springs of character; commerce, which one of the brilliant orators of Europe called the "locomotive of principles;" which always has in it a profounder significance than the dumb merchandise it handles, packs, ships, and computes profits on, — involving, as it does, the eternal principles of ethics in its exchanges, — the occult laws of political economy and celestial charity in its distribution, and binding the tribes of the earth together by cords of mutual traffic first, that it may bind them in Christian brotherhood afterwards. God's strength has reared its warehouses in all open ports, for character. God's bounty has freighted its thousand holds; his permission has loosened its cables and slid its navies from so many opposite harbors into the expanse of so many seas; his steadfastness has held its anchors fast; his breath has pressed its sails, and balanced its keels, and hardened its masts, and pointed the needle of its compass, and braced the sinews of its mariners; his care has made all elements further it,—the winds and the fire to speed it, and, from the hollow of his own hand, has poured afresh forever the waters that float it; God's nourishment has grown the forests that have been bent into its knees; God's eye has followed the track of its every vessel, on all oceans and straits,—in the chafings of Arctic ice, where Humanity has searched the barren promontories for signals of its lost explorers, or under equatorial skies, where it opens the doors of both the Indies to the enterprise of both the continents; —and all this, not for mouths, or bodies, or tax-bills, or banks, but for the soul of man, and because he is a social being.

Very largely we are a commercial people, and also an educated people. Need it be told, then, how human equity, human forbearance, human justice, human industry, human energy, get their daily discipline in the bargainings, the partnerships, the commissions, the exchanges of that business? how God would have men merchants, that they may recognize the obligation of mercantile fidelity as surely as their navigation does its magnet and currents; keep their credit as even as its tides; and open their charities as wide as its seas?

Then, when commercial disaster comes,—when men

see the walls of their fortunes closing in, and high-built estates tumble and crash till all confidence shakes, and starving multitudes mourn the ruin, and crime rushes in to snatch its guilty harvest by violence,—when stout hearts fail for fear, and friends look into each other's faces only to read there suspicion and alarm,—when strong men go home at night to wake and weep, and when capitalists and bankers, used to ease, and lovers of life, as they turn their locks in the morning, say, "Would God it were evening," and meanness fattens on distress, and honor dreads loss of faith more than loss of millions, —shall I undertake to say, Who then speaks, and who shall be still? You have heard the voice for yourselves. Time, and suffering, and thought, and prayer, slowly offer the interpretation; and this they say plainly,—that God's Providence is the preceptor, and character the lesson.

V. There are *local* forms of Society. The most imposing of these, a representative of all the rest, the structure that commerce builds, is a great city. Not more true is it that since the days of Nineveh, Phœnicia, Tyre, Carthage, the wary eyes of statesmen and political economists have always been fixed on metropolitan peoples as the springs and seats of political movement, than that the eye of moral insight sees there the most vivid and thrilling encounter of all the forces of humanity. Stretching out the tentacula of its traffic, till, in coarser or finer filaments, they encircle the globe; fed, through port and avenue, by every climate; ornamented by the ingenuity of every country's genius; bearing no blade of grass, yet piling wealth to the sky; answering with quick, responsive sympathies to every exciting breath that stirs anywhere the air of the world, remember, that tumultuous mass of life, congregated, multitudinous, is yet made up of individual units, — souls that the whole is strengthening or corrupting, sanctifying or cursing, for eternity. What the curious gazer beholds, when he places himself by the street-side, and watches the changing faces that pass, in strange exhibition, before him, stamped each with some new expression, — with sorrow or a smile, with anxiety or cheerfulness, with thought or feeling, with listlessness or eagerness, is but an emblem of all the city is and represents. As there are light-hearted and laughing companies following hard upon funeral processions; as disease walks arm in arm with health, and wretchedness in rags marches in locked steps with luxury, — so in the deep reality of the spirit. By contrasts and conflicts like these, in your palaces, your decent dwellings, your dens,—in your decorated paganism and your impoverished glory,—in the gorgeous temple of the Pharisee and the publican's holier corner, God visits you every morning and tries you every moment, besets you literally behind and before, and lays his hand upon you.

"Let me move slowly through the street,
Filled with an everlasting train,
Amid the sound of steps that beat
The murmuring walks, like autumn rain.

"Youth, with pale cheek and slender frame,
And dreams of greatness in thine eye,
Goest thou to build an early name,
Or early in thy tasks to die?

"Keen son of trade, with eager brow,
Who is now fluttering in thy snare?
Thy golden fortunes,—tower they now,
Or melts the glittering shape in air?

"Who of this crowd, to-night, shall tread
The dance till daylight gleams again?
Who sorrow o'er the untimely dead?
Who writhe, themselves, in mortal pain?

"Each, where his tasks or pleasures call,
They pass and heed each other not.
There is Who heeds, who holds them all,
In his large love and boundless thought.

"These struggling tides of life that seem
In shifting, aimless course to tend,
Are eddies of the mighty stream
That rolls to its predestined end."*

* Bryant.

Yes; that busy human hive is more than a master-piece of superb mercantile mechanism; more than a facility of subsistence, show and gain; more than a vast hotel for the migrating trains that people and till the hemispheres. It is a discipline of human souls. For still, "at the entry of the city, Wisdom cries, 'Unto you, O man, I call.'"

The question, so much debated, between the moral advantages or securities, on the whole, of city and country, is capable of no conclusion,—because the two are not in the relations of an alternative, but are needful parts of a complete variety. For instance, refinement, which is best bred in metropolitan manners, because of the observation, opportunity, and examples not possibly accumulated elsewhere, is an actual good. So is a certain reserved individuality, held in a forcible and contemplative equipoise, an actual good; and that is best bred off the pavements. Men's reasonings in this matter are very apt to run according to their tastes, and so their conclusions represent only their preferences. It is said, for example, that the rural attachment and bond to the soil is a source of the spirit of liberty: but, on the other hand, history seems to show that independence of prescription and prerogative has often broken out, and held sway, in commercial cities; while we, as descendants from a British ancestry, know something of the tenacity and arrogance of a landed aristocracy. Considering the absence of interruption and mixture, it has been naturally alleged that country life is favorable to profound reflection, and the thorough assimilating of whatever knowledge is acquired. But then it is found that in order to this effect the prior condition of mental activity is necessary; and a purely agricultural community almost always grows heavy and stolid in a few generations unless it is quickened and stirred by some contact with great centres. Then, it is just as true, and indeed it is proverbial, how the too imitative and too luxurious and too superficial propensities of most cities require that the stock of native vigor and moral earnestness should be often replenished from the unworn energy of the fields and the mountains. The inference is not obscure. Each of these scenes has its own faults, limitations, and depravities. And in the complete structure of civilization, where producing, carrying, modifying the raw material, or manufacturing and exchanging, are the great modes of the public economy, social wants and supplies spring up in both, which are naturally adapted to each other.

VI. We might take, as another instance, the popular assembly. Who that, in periods of public emotion, has stood in a crowded congregation and felt the enthusiasm kindle, mounting sometimes to frenzy, as sympathies spring and react, glow and rise, are reflected, reverberated, redoubled; who that has marked their effect not only on forensic eloquence but on practical enterprises, from the days of the Athenian agora to our modern platforms; who that has watched their fearful approaches to revolutionary terror and insurrectionary demonism, as they degenerate from deliberative counsel to the riot and the mob, — needs be told how often humanity in the individual is the ready pupil of humanity in the mass?

VII. Indeed, the whole of that power in communities that is named public opinion, is one of the most significant exhibitions of the social sentiment in its action on the citizen. It is the accumulated pressure of an aggregate, bearing down on each of the constituents. What we call fashion, in all its forms, is only a kind of dramatizing of public opinion, — the average preference dominating the personal judgment, or giving a momentum to indifference. Mighty for beneficence when it is in the right, it is just as mighty for mischief when perverted. It is a sifter of the stuff men are made of. If it crooks the supple hinges of many knees, it finds others whose sinews cannot be bent,—

only their bread withheld, or their blood spilt; and then the next age crowns them as its heroes. If it entices some to put their principles into the market, so it meets others not saleable at any price, who say to its seductions, "Get thee behind me, Satan," and are lifted up thereby at once, and have angels come and minister to them. Even where there is no "divinity hedging about the person of a king," there is the patronage of a majority for the ambitious, the bait of popularity, the charm of favoring winds, — tests of positive manhood. Then, when policy and self-interest have stolen the livery of Justice and Patriotism,—when the sordid greed for place hath conceived and brought forth every civil sin, — when the rule of political proceeding is to put certain labelled candidates in, right or wrong, and to keep certain branded candidates out, wrong or right,—then is the time for individual virtue to prove its breeding, for good men to stand forth, for brave men to breast the current; then shall ye discern between him that serveth God and him that serveth him not. By the very pressure of its own perils, Society reconstructs its own order.

We gather, now, the general tendency of these several illustrations of our main proposition, that

Society is a Discipline of Individual Character, and thus an agent of the Divine Disposition,—as we have noticed them in various forms of Social Life,—the family, the relation of employer and employed, the general intercourse of company, commerce, a city, a public assembly, and popular opinion. In each of these fields we have sought examples of two great laws, viz., a reciprocal relation and inter-dependence of all social and personal life, with a reflex effect of all outward moral action on the soul that produces it.*

It will naturally and practically conclude this survey, if you will bring before you some single soul's history, to witness how its career is wrought out, and its moral elements are mingled, by its immersion in the social atmosphere, and its giving and taking with other persons. Start with it at its starting-point. See how it gathered from parents, from brothers and sisters, from playmates, from school-companions, from neighbors, from all the faces it met, from all the talk it heard, from all the temperatures that burnt or chilled it. It is

* "*Things* have no society, or capacity of social relations. In mere nature, considered as a mere scheme of cause and effect, there is nothing social, any more than there is in the members of a steam engine. Love, benefit, sympathy, injury, hatred, thanks, blame, character, worship, faith, all that constitutes the reality of Society, belong to the fact that we are consciously powers."—BUSHNELL.

often lamented, what a diffusive pestilence has crept out upon our English literature, and into thousands of private lives, from the looser pages of one unprincipled genius. But few who deplore Byron's terribly prostituted faculty, go behind his own morbid, misanthropic sensuality, to watch the moulding influence of the passionate, unscrupulous mother who first woke the fury in his bosom. The unfeeling taunts of her mortified vanity at one physical deformity in his person, her bitter sarcasms, her angry maledictions, dropped on his susceptible childhood, in the retirements of their home, like poison on a plant, and the corroded germ shot into a baleful manhood, blighting the world's purity far more than it beautified its poetry. There is no exhausting the capacity of character to take the mould of every social type it meets. Whatever human stuff we touch cleaves to our fingers. If it is the pitch of sin, we are defiled. If it is the alabaster-box of precious virtues, we carry the fragrant anointing to our burial. So we "build each other up." Every living soul you ever met, since your mother bent over your new-born life, has wrought its effect,—slight, unseen, imperceptible, very often, yet blessing or blasting,—on your being and your destiny.

The shadows of apostles, passing by, shed their

silent virtue on the sick laid by the wayside. Some nameless influence, be it inspiration, be it temptation, has gone out from your least conscious hours, and by word, by look, by tone, by gesture, by repulsion or attraction, by stimulus or depression, has altered and shaped in its little measure every child, man, woman, you ever knew. Most terrible trust! "If thou knewest," exclaims Richter,* "that every black thought of thine, or every glorious independent one, separated itself from thy soul, and took root outside of thee, and for half a century," — oh, infinitely longer than that! — "pushed and bore its poisonous or healing roots, oh how piously wouldst thou choose and think!"

The ancients assigned to the banks of an imaginary lake, lying at the entrance of the veiled Hereafter, a court of forty-two judges, to pass on the fitness of the candidates for immortality. But our God, who is One, and a Spirit, has set Society itself, in all its countless members, for our perpetual judgment, by those everlasting principles, Power, Justice, Goodness, which he has appointed Society to embody, teach, and spread. And when the veil of things outward, which now partly obscures the workings of these divine laws, shall finally be lifted, then will rise up again the long train of spirits,

* "Doctrine of Education."

tempters or helpers, with accusation, with benediction. One will say, in tones of sadness and agony which no dramatic art can prophesy, "It was of you I learned my first oath, and because of you oaths afterwards grew familiar to my lips as household words." Another, "Of you I learned to defile my imagination with unclean shapes, till the pollution grew thick on my heart as slime on filthy pools." Another, "But for you, dishonesty would have been a hateful mystery to me for ever; your cunning seduced my honor." Another, "It was you that, by the exasperating word, spoken at the beginning of strife, and thence spinning its long trail of vexation down the walls of my peace, fretted my natural petulance into ungovernable wrath and irretrievable crime." Another still, "Your worldly levity quenched my holier purposes, just when the striving Spirit was calling me up to consecration and to Christ." Thus, by the power of our social nature, working on with rigorous consistency to the end, the very victims of our thoughtless indulgence come to wield the scourges of our retribution. Shall it not be that some grateful soul, speaking out of the multitude that no man can number, having the Father's name in his forehead, and the new white stone in his hand, with the new name that no man knoweth saving he that receiveth it, shall say, "Praise be to God! not unto us: not, O man, unto thee! But thy faithful counsel, thy frank word, thy charitable deed, thy unpretending prayer, reached after me, touched me, delivered me, inspired me, saved me?"

There is bondage in the conspiracies of sin. There is freedom in the fellowship of the good. Out of the one the soul goes leprous, like Miriam, pale with the ghastly disorder of guilt. From the other it goes, as from the Mount of Transfiguration, clothed with light falling from the saintly glory of Moses and Elias. And if He who is greater than Moses, and has more than the spirit and power of Elias, has been found there, then, in the homes and hospitalities of Society, God will have made his tabernacles with men, and, disciplined by their heavenly economy, individual man will render back his noble contributions to the spiritual wealth of the world.

LECTURE IV.

SOCIETY A SCHOOL OF MUTUAL HELP.

In treating Human Society as a method of divine discipline for individual character, we adverted, among other bearings of that subject, to the energy and diversity of action into which the social principle unfolds the affections. Leading out of that line of thought, yet distinct enough from it to justify a separate discussion, is the doctrine of mutual assistance. The Father of men has so related the various parts and pursuits and interests of Society, that they move forward to the best fulfilment of all their several objects, and wind together into the most majestic harmonies, in proportion as they act and react, with reciprocal ministries of good, upon each other. No aspect of our human kind yields ampler or brighter proofs of God's intentions than this.

It is a matter of simple observation, and very familiar, that wherever a number of people are thrown together for a common object, even for a short period, in such conditions that the entertainment of each depends directly upon the good-will of the whole, there acquaintance ripens fast, and friends for life are made in a day. Parties of pleasure at the sea-shore, companies of fellow-travellers on a long journey, where the conventional forms are waived for the sake of immediate enjoyment, put all our tedious drawing-room etiquette, and our elaborate apparatus of ceremonial intercourse,—as a means, *i. e.*, of getting human hearts together,—into the shade, at once. The same effect accrues wherever people are assembled, on the sudden outbreak of some peril or actual calamity. An unexpected joy, or escape, if it were only vivid enough to tear through the prevailing crust of formality, would serve just as well. There is, it is true, a tradition of a French master of manners, who apologized for letting another gentleman drown before his eyes without offering the assistance that would easily have saved him, because such an interference would have been a breach of politeness, as he had never had the pleasure of being introduced to that gentleman's acquaintance,—an instance of the detriment man takes from his artificial conventions. But, exceptions apart, those occurrences that act powerfully on the strong emotions in us, break up reserve and draw and bind people together. It results from the law that a community of feeling in the greater interest of Humanity, supersedes the discrimination and separation in the less. And it is only a more salient illustration of that underlying bond of mutual dependency and assistance which runs through the constitution of man, and links into one all the members of the social body.

I say *all* the members. For, in considering Society as we do now, it is the very beauty of the truth before us that it takes up every individual specimen of the race. It includes the least noticed, the least active, the most obscure. It gathers in the unreckoned and latent forces of humanity,—not merely a few conspicuous persons, or a privileged class. A French writer estimates that of the thirty-six millions of that nation, only ten millions really enter into the ideas that lie at the foundation of the government,—the rest being indifferent. The proportion will vary among the nations. But these outlying masses are not omitted from the contemplation of the principle of mutual assistance before us. Politics may overlook them; God never. All are still members of Society, and are acting and reacting on one another. More or less freely, more or less blindly, more or less unconsciously, they are working together for each other's relief and furtherance,—since God is working over and within them all. Social perfection is not merely a bending of others' wills to our own, nor yet merely a sacrifice of ours to theirs. It is a subordination of all beside to the highest end of the whole, — not the greatest happiness but the greatest goodness of all. And it is towards that, only by slow, stumbling, and often painful steps, not without occasional retrogradations of tyranny and hatred, that God has appointed Society to make its way.

Notice that the principle continues to operate, whether individual dispositions conform to it consciously, or consciously rebel at it. As was said before, allowance must be made for the personal liberty of choice. The original design may be thwarted, but never baffled. Somebody resists, and goes down. The eternal Thought moves on, undisturbed and sublime. If then we see the social design slowly and steadily fulfilled, in spite of the selfish opposition, if the social laws hold out, overbearing, in the long run, private plans, it is only a more signal attestation of the ruling mind of the Maker.

Without a very formal division, the fields from which I shall seek my principal instances, in the discussion and application of the great principle, will be those of the benevolent sympathies, the relations of sex, productive industry, the trades, nations.

Let us, at the outset, test the doctrine, in two

extreme cases: one a social relation where the two parties present the least that is mutual in appearance or in condition, which is casual, and may sometime pass away altogether; the other a relation which is as permanent as the race, essential to the species, but where the very organic character of the distinction creates a peculiar difficulty in adjusting the rule of reciprocity. I mean, first, the relation of helpless penury to property; secondly, the relation of woman to man.

If there is any class where the law fails, we should probably say, at first thought, it must be among the poor, who seem to have nothing to give back for what they receive. Indeed, we have a curious evidence of that fallacy in our use of language; for we call those who take the gift *beneficiaries*, as if the only benefit were with them. Arrayed in fashion's costume, out of fortune's wardrobe, wheeling our luxurious couches up to the blazing grate of a winter's night, we discourse complacently and self-righteously of the annoying mendicants that will come beggared to our gates, —of their frauds, lies, impositions,—forgetting that as many frauds and lies and impositions went, first and last, possibly, to the furnishing of our handsome apartments, or may be seen and heard by the Almighty inside of them; forgetting, also.

that we owe gratitude and favor to these wretched creatures who wait for our mercy, because they call up a momentary thrill of pity in our world-bound hearts, and so save us from the very barbarism of prosperity. Yes: the rich have to thank the poor, with just as much reason as the poor the rich. Character is moulded into its best proportions as much by what is done for others, as by what is taken from them. It is mutual help. Indeed, this is the test that discriminates all alms-givings: do they benefit one party only, or both? do they only feed and clothe starvation's body, or the giver's spirit as well? Is not your soul as likely to starve from selfishness, as the beggar's body for want of bread? There are poorer men than I am, to the end that I may make myself freely poorer for their sake; and that will be my most godlike privilege.* Taking from me earthly things, they pour back spiritual things. Taking clothing or food, they give patience, cheerfulness, love, faith, and a power to bear my own crosses. Every poor child, really in want, or ignorant, that ever stretched out a hand to you for help, has been a part of God's discipline with you. He has exercised a divine ministry upon you. Before God you can never be again as if that slender, suppli-

* 2 Corinthians, viii. 9.

cating arm had not once been lifted in your path. It will come back, in the strange quickenings of memory, in fever, or midnight, or the last judgment. A debt rose up upon you; and better or worse you will be — better you were meant to be — for eternity. I think you all must have noticed that persons who spent much time in really and heartily helping others had their moral eyesight purified and even their intellect brightened. Their whole nature grows firm, and calm, and vigorous, and wise. By the expansion their presence thus gives to our moral horizon, a needy family, first entangling our sympathies in their straitened lot, set our feet finally in a larger place, and become our richest creditors. Lazarus comes a prophet of regeneration to Dives' gate. Penury preaches salvation from its ragged pulpit, in the name of him who had not where to lay his head, and who, in his own blessed person, made poverty sacred forever. Silver and gold these children of a new apostleship have not, but none the less it may be a gate called "Beautiful" where we meet them, for they loosen and uplift our crippled affections, and we too go healed, leaping and walking and praising, to the temple.

Again, both the friendly design of nature, and the gross contempt of it by false philanthropy, are pronounced with particular emphasis in the case of the most permanent, marked and indispensable of all the social distinctions of the Human Race—that of the two sexes. Here, again, see the social balance, in its most striking shape,—variety of constitution, with unity of moral design,—a mutuality. That woman is not yet fulfilling her whole rightful work in the social economy, is obvious to common sense. The real relative rights of the two sexes will be settled, only when each enjoys the liberty of unfolding and exercising its own peculiar character, whatever it may be, suffering no obstruction or hindrance from the other. Now, the whole group of human faculties, intellectual, moral and spiritual—make what enumeration or classification of them you please—unquestionably belong to both these sexes. The difference is in their relative proportions and adjustments. And the reason of that difference must have been the balance and harmony of unlike powers, prevailing throughout creation. Of course, you realize nature's intention, not by approximating to masculine women, or feminine men, but by giving each sex its own distinctive place, and developing each to the greatest capacity in itself, and the greatest help of the other. In that distinction of relative proportions, the *distinguishing* faculty of the male sex is mental concentration; that of the female is moral impulse. Woman, when she is truly *womanly*, carries her special strength in her heart; man, when he is truly *manly*, carries his strength in his head. Neither monopolizes the special department; but, by eminence, he is reason, she is love. Woman, however powerfully she may think—and in some instances she will think more powerfully than man—is the representative of affection. Man, however ardently and constantly he may love—and in some instances he will love more ardently and more constantly than woman—is the representative of thought. If any of us think this discrimination gives any advantage to man, it is only because we are not yet Christian enough to acknowledge that spirit is grander than intellect, holiness wiser than logic, the human heart deeper and nobler than the head.

But the point here is, that each is really most honored, most advanced, most benefitted, exactly when the other is; so that the whole debate about their respective "rights," or, worse yet, their comparative merits, becomes both unphilosophical and vulgar. The simple constitution of their being,—the primitive record of God's creative act, "male and female created he them," ought to have foreclosed, forever, that impertinent strife. Whichever way the controversy should be decided, the decision would be wrong. You might as well inquire which of any two of the great essential elements of existence, or laws of matter, is most important. You might as well ask, respecting any of those grand dualities, between which the sublime order of nature is poised and unity is held fast, which could best be spared. You might as well discuss the comparative merits of morning and evening, of the bones and the blood, of the centrifugal and centripetal forces, of the systole and diastole of the heart, of the negative and positive electrical poles, of the green of the earth and the blue of the sky. Each holds its title by the ordaining of a divine plan; and the displacement of either from its sphere would be a resolution of the system into chaos. The whole dispute is a monstrous anomaly, conceived in an unnatural jealousy, protracted by an insane insurrection against good manners, and sure to end in nothing but a profane putting asunder of what God hath joined together. For wherever either sex is truly best, strongest, happiest, there the other must be.*

* "A family,—than which there is no more genuine type of nature's method of arrangement,—is throughout a combination of *opposites;* the woman depending on the man, whose very strength, however, exists only by her weakness; the child hanging on the parent, whose power were no blessing, were it not compelled to stoop in gentleness; the brother protecting the sister, whose affections would have but half their wealth, were they not brought to lean on him with trustful pride: and even among seeming equals, the impetuous quieted by the thought-

Proceed now to observe some of the external methods and instruments of the mutual social assistance. Perhaps the most common are the productive pursuits and every-day labors of men. There again, as in the case of the sexes, it is by the law of social diversity, reciprocity, and balance, that the grandest results are worked out.

ful, and the timid finding shelter with the brave. That there 'are diversities of gifts' is the reason why there 'is one spirit:' and it is because one is reliable for knowledge, and another for resolve, and a third for the graces of a balanced mind, that all are held in the bonds of a pure affection.

"The same principle distinguishes natural society from artificial association. The former, springing from the impulse of human feeling, brings together elements that are unlike: the latter, directed to specific ends, combines the like. The one, completing defect by redundance, and compensating redundance by defect, produces a real and living unity; the other, multiplying a mere fraction of life by itself, retires further and further from any integral good, and results only in exaggerated partiality. I do not suppose that society arises, as some philosophers represent, from the sense of individual weakness, and the desire for consolidated strength; but, it must be owned, the instinctive propensities of mankind create nearly the same natural classes as if it were so. So long as personal qualities and spontaneous attractions determine the sorting of mankind, they will dispose themselves in classes, containing each, in rugged harmony, the elementary materials of our humanity. And when discord arises, it is from the presence of too many similar elements, which have no respect for one another, no mutual want, no reciprocal helpfulness, and which cannot, therefore, coëxist without risk of dissension. Say what you will, nature is no democrat, but filled throughout with ranks; and it is only in proportion as we recede from the natural affections, and enter upon the life of isolated self-will, that dreams of social equality take place of the reality of social obedience."—Rev. James Martineau.

The same principle holds of professions and trades as of persons. These pursuits enter into their "holy alliance" when they blend the two aims,—to improve themselves and help one another. "The carpenter encourages the blacksmith, and he that smootheth with the hammer him that smites the anvil." While men and women are Good Samaritans, it never was meant that their employments should be priests and Levites, nor trippers and pirates. The commonwealth is not served, till the different branches of industry merge their jealousies in good-will.

The very composition of the earth we walk over offers a strong hint of this intention. You read it in the beautiful balancings of clouds and tides, the equations of astronomy, the adjustments of growths and climate,—all the musical accord by which the Divine Spirit has attuned his creation to an everlasting anthem. Sky and water, vapor and vegetation, earth and sun, are ever friendly and hospitable; they are perpetually running on some missionary errand in each other's behalf. Their Bureau of Benevolence is older than the Holy College. The gates of their hospitality, like the Bukharian nobleman's, are "nailed open." They preach the creed of Brotherhood in that temple whose roof is fretted with the stars.

Indeed, it is most interesting to see how liberally the Creator has given hints and illustrations of this social principle, by his own arrangements, even in what we call the humbler departments of his creation. For Society does not stand apart from Nature, but interlinks its laws with hers. Very wonderful it is, and very beautiful, to see how God twines together, into a system of mutual benefits, the operations that different creatures carry on for their own advantage, thus revealing his intention that they should be fellow-helpers,—even these dumb and soulless things. He scarcely lets any good end with the being that produced it, but carries it over into some wider usefulness. He pushes out the doings of each animal and person into results that help other animals and other persons. The silkworm, with no thought of a charity, spins for himself an elaborate and complicated coffin, to hold the chrysalis, till its resurrection with wings. But the strands of that delicate fabric, the ingenuity of man winds off into the material of his costliest and most durable vestures. Coral insects build their reefs with the slow toil of ages, not certainly as philanthropists, but simply by the instinct that bids living things provide a habitation. Yet they are all the time laying the foundations of islands that men will sometime inhabit, when overpopulated continents shall send out their swarming colonies, and thus God "layeth the beams of his chambers in the waters." The spider weaves a web, out in the air, for certain economical purposes of his own. But God bathes it overnight in drops of dew, and in the morning sun it hangs like a silver shield, with miniature rainbows for its quarterings, "a thing of beauty" at which children clap their hands with rapture, and which every beauty-loving passenger is the better for. The spider had no thought of being an artist; but the Creator made him one to shed delight unconsciously. Or else Astronomy stretches one of these slender fibres across the glass in her telescope to mark the passage of a star, and the little insect under a clover leaf gives a measuring line to science to tell the august motions of the constellations of the sky.

So in another and higher grade of creation.

When men forget to help each other, God overrules their plans, and makes them do it, to a certain extent, in despite of themselves. He circumvents the sharpest calculation, and outwits the shrewdest diplomacy. He is forever defeating the plots of selfishness. He suffers no immunities to be strictly personal. It is the settled policy of Providence, so to speak, to break up monopolies. He regards always the good, not only of the greatest number, but of the whole. He allows no mortal to live for himself alone, however much disposed to. A capitalist, without the remotest intention of being a public benefactor perhaps, founds a factory, to enlarge his private fortune. But the enterprise calls into employment an army of laborers, and the wages forestall their starvation. A few men, in a corporation, as the case may be, build a railway, for the sake of the dividends; but it becomes an immeasurable facility of travel and transportation, and while it enriches a few is a convenience to millions. An insurance office is established for the profit of the stockholders, or the salary of the officers, but it turns out to be a general help. Adventurers sail in search of foreign gold, and dig it out of the mud for their own aggrandizement. But nature, with no thought of that, uses these precious ores to ease the tightened money pressure and help the finances of the whole trading world. A merchant may, if he will, hem round his wealth by every possible barrier, shut it up in investments, in banks, in loans of exorbitant interest; let him hold it with never so desperate a grasp, some of it, less or more, will leak out and run over and get into circulation for the general good. He must have clerks to keep his growing accounts; he must have draymen to handle his merchandise; he must have factors and agents to manage his great machine, or else it will clog and break, and they must have their share. He would do it all and keep it all himself possibly, if he could, but Providence has limited his capacity, given him but one pair of hands, a fixed faculty of attention, and only twenty-four hours to a day. He must employ operatives; he must help his fellows, though it be against his will. If he loves display and indulgence, then he must support upholsterers and the markets. No credit to him; but it shows God's law.

He discovers the same law, historically. British taxation was not *meant* to help the American colonies, only to relieve the English exchequer. But the spirit it roused has sent civilization forward with a mightier impulse than it had felt for ages before. On the whole, the oppression proved a very considerable help, not only to America but to the world. The march of Alexander's armies opened highways across the East in which peaceful industries and improvements both followed and obliterated the devastations of war. Heaven made even the fierce Macedonian phalanx the pioneer of Humanity, and used that bloody scourge, their leader, whose gluttony hungered after more worlds than one to conquer, as a helper to the oriental nations. Vespasian's Roman cohorts, aflame with military lust, had no idea of spreading the mild faith of Christ or of helping men; they sought only to complete the dominion of the empire, when they bore their victorious arms to Palestine, and planted their standards about the holy city. But that very ruin levelled the Temple worship, spread one language for Truth to speak in, and Christendom was helped. The downfall of the Ritual was the inauguration of the Gospel. The hoarse voice of havoc ended in the gentle breathing forth, all over the eastern world, of the Messiah's compassion. William of Normandy can hardly be reckoned among the voluntary helpers of Humanity. He invaded England and conquered the Saxon, for the love of power. But he was made an involuntary helper. For that invasion broke up the old system of vassalage, introduced into English society that stalwart middle class out of which has come all that is noblest and brightest in the national character, — Magna Charta, Parliamentary Reform, Shakespeare's tragedies, the Puritan Reformation, Paradise Lost, and a commerce that belts the globe. Help out of injury; this is everywhere the method of God.

My next position is, that the same divine intention is manifest, and the same lesson is taught, in the fact that throughout creation this system of mutual assistance is made necessary from the mutual dependence that obtains everywhere. Each depends on each, and each on the whole. The several kingdoms of nature depend on and therefore help each other. The mineral is the solid basis on which is spread out the vegetable, — the body that its vesture clothes. The vegetable directly nourishes the animal. The tree does not grow for itself; it cradles the birds, and feeds animated races, and shades the traveller till he blesses it. Of all the ninety thousand species of plants that Botany has classified, not one, from the vast oak to the weed that springs out of its mould and the moss that clings to its bark, but takes its appointed place in a related family. The atmosphere would lose its salubrity but for the salt and bitter sea. The ground would catch no fertilizing streams if the clouds did not kindly drop them from the sky. The flowers wait for the falling light before they unveil their beauty. All growing things are buttressed up by the vast ribs of everlasting granite that sleep in sunless caverns. Heat, electricity, magnetism, attraction, send their subtle powers through nature, and play through all its works, as unseen and silent as the eternal spirit they bear witness of. Everything helps. Everything is helped.

This dependence, too, is still more striking in human life. The trades exemplify it. Precisely because no one man can reach perfection in all the arts, and be a proficient in every profession, the progress of civilization requires the division of labor; not division in the sense of hostility, but a division of works with a common will,—many departments with one interest, "diversities of operation with the same spirit." Not more completely does the wheel of the engine depend upon the boiler, or the rod upon the valve, than one individual upon another in the more intricate and wondrous mechanism of Society. Every business reaches its perfection by the concentrated devotion of one mind; and this man, meantime, must be supported by other pursuits in other hands. The hands divide, but they are still fellow-helpers. While each toils at his own bench, he is really working for all the rest, and all the rest for him. Society is like a great manufacturing establishment I have seen, where some hundreds of workmen are employed, yet the results of the skill of all, in all departments, are combined and blended together in the product, which is a musical instrument. So there may be moral harmony out of industrial distribution. The old fable of the blind man and the cripple is realized every day. Every man has some gift or opportunity that another has not. Both the blind and the lame are helpless alone. But once establish a mutual relation of dependence and help between them, and then the blind man can take up the cripple, and the cripple, borne on his companion's shoulders, is eyes to the blind. There is a profound meaning in this simple parable. Every person in the world is under some infirmity,—blind or lame,—if alone. Would each man carry his own power of usefulness to its highest pitch, with a single will, but with a generous breast, then the royal law of Society would be fulfilled.

> "Heaven forming each on other to depend,
> A master, or a servant, or a friend,
> Bids each on other for assistance call,
> Till one man's weakness grows the strength of all."

We find another impressive illustration of this social interdependence in the fact that, as fast as any one productive pursuit is perfected, the rest incline to share in the benefits of that completeness. Science helps art; the arts help each other; machinery helps commerce, and commerce helps literature. They all prepare each other's tools, refine each other's materials, sharpen each other's wits, raise each other's standards, and, in a thousand ways, multiply mutual facilities. The surgeon can practice more clean and skilful clinics, if the cutler was skilful before him. The chemist is indebted to the glass-blower, and the glass-blower to the coal-heaver, and the coal-heaver to the basket-maker. What were your commerce without the paper-maker and the ship-builder? There is no kind of manufacturing, and hardly a family, that has not reaped as substantial profits from the modern elaborations of mechanism, or of the elastic gums, as the proprietors have. By better castings in metals a whole cluster of arts is set forward. Every calling reaches over to drop a blessing on its relatives. One prepares instruments and accessories for another. Agriculture wants the college for its analyses and scientific suggestions. What a short-sighted envy, if the farmer tries to embarrass and disendow the university! The college wants agriculture for its produce, its patronage, its pupils. What a vulgar prejudice, if the collegian sneers at the farmer! How clearly God designs to press forward and upward all the complicated interests of mankind together; making each the better for the others, affording a splendid example of his own unifying providence, and making all to crystallize into an orderly organization, and thus to work out the gradual reconcilement of Society.

So, if one member suffer, all the members,—not only by voluntary sympathy, but by God's law inwrought in them,—suffer with it. It is said that if a milch cow breaks her leg, her milk instantly loses its lime, which is taken off to cement the fracture and restore the wounded limb. Bruise or break one limb of the social body, and the whole vital secretion grows thin and sour. At the bottom all our business is one. Down at the roots of the world our roots all interlace. It is one wide subsoil of humanity that sends up so many shapes and colors, and after all, with all its shifting weather and varied climates, our planet knows only the experience of one toiling, throbbing, loving heart.

By bringing men together you reconcile them. Even amidst the injustices and violences of slavery, the body-slaves are observed to be privileged, and tenderly treated,—a certain power of the human quality breaking down the temper of caste and the barriers of pride.

You are shut up half an hour in a stage-coach, or crowded into the corner of a drawing-room, with the whig or democrat against whom you were just ready to launch, the next morning, a bitter political pamphlet; and you go home and burn the manuscript, or at least strike out the adjectives, and, ennobled by your humanized manners, exult in the determination never again to let party differences disturb social relations. The divine workmanship is nowhere self-contradictory. History is

God's discourse, as Society is his living illustration, and the conclusion never contradicts the exordium. The moment mankind truly understand one another, they will be at peace. In order to this mutual acquaintance, the social communications must be multiplied, and the social sympathies quickened, which is exactly the business of Society. We never do truly know one another till we feel each other's feelings, and aspire with one another's aspirations, as well as think each other's thoughts. So with the great tribes of men. Let the Russian soul actually appreciate the Turkish soul, and hostilities must cease. But before that can be, both their souls must be larger. At present their proportions are too meagre to support a right manly life in themselves; how can you expect them to contain one another's? What you want, to end a quarrel, is only to let the belligerents see each other's human nature; and, to that end, to get them a human nature large enough to be seen, and to take in something broader than a selfish interest. In other words, there must be, in these repugnant races, a more generous social culture, and a better development of humanity; a larger quantity of the real human being. So the world over. The reason the trades and sciences do not agree better, is that they do not know each other's bearings and relations. Let them see that the perfecting of each is the prosperity of all. Two of our great American productive forces, — our agriculture and our manufactures,—have not yet come into a good, amicable, neighborly understanding. They are like two suspicious and sharp-eyed housekeepers that happen to move into adjoining houses. They sit at their windows, watch each other's movements, criticise each other's housekeeping, and gossip with their respective friends over each other's management, till they have matured a very satisfactory hatred. But when they have been fairly introduced, at some sudden emergency, like a fire, or a nativity, and have sat down to talk matters over, they are transformed into the most confidential of companions. The moment you bring the Factory and the Farm to a thorough reciprocal intelligence, you solve the whole problem of the tariff, because you demonstrate to both parties that they are not two interests but one. And either one grows by the other.*

Blunders are constantly perpetrated in our social economy, and our attempts at reform, by this partial information, due to our one-sided develop-

* See an eloquent passage in Ruskin's "Political Economy of Art," page 160, etc. See also Adam Ferguson's "Civil Society," Part iv., section i.

ment, and sluggishness of thought. We try to judge the wants of the world from our little post of private observation. We apply help, but in the wrong spot. We complicate, instead of relieving, the difficulty. We offer to the poor what *we* like, instead of what *they need*, and so feed their wastefulness instead of their economy and their moral courage. The poor must be fed; in the present state of social knowledge and attainment, it is as much the dictate of self-preservation as of benevolence to feed them outright. Rousseau was right, "When the poor have nothing to eat, they will eat the rich." It is terribly true. But after a Christianized science has properly arranged the whole social structure, and effected a just distribution of industry and privilege, alms will more and more give place to wages. Charity will find its exercise, not in the gross supply of empty stomachs, but in the higher and more beautiful offices that minister moral sympathy and spiritual strength. The different classes will really help and strengthen one another, just as fast as they all contribute to a science of universal growth. Carpenter and goldsmith, lawyer and shipwright, farmer and fisherman, help every one his neighbor, only as they all join to open and illustrate and publish the grand laws of human effort and providential equity.

We have next to observe the action of this law of reconciliation in those great communities of men called nations, or their governments. When we have gone to the bottom of the matter, whether by the way of philosophy or Christianity, we shall find that the fundamental idea of politics is mutual protection and friendly intercourse. I do not say this is the idea of feudal or aristocratic or imperial or partisan politics, but of the true, ultimate, divine politics — towards which all these are tentative experiments. Not to hold each other back, and pull each other down, and rob, and stab, but to confederate for the common good, and to complete, by means of equal labor and free energies, an economy of universal production whereof all shall take the benefit,—this is the real and providential office, whether of separate empires, or of the several departments under the same administration. Hence, you serve the cause of good government, both when you perfect any legitimate business as one of the great nutritious forces which feed and cover humanity, and also when you bring that business into amity and reciprocity with other kinds of business. Unless God fails to furnish a pattern for his children in his own love, the right *political* state for mankind is the state of social help.

According to this higher view of international

connections, whatever forwards the growth of one government is a service to all. England, in such a state of things, suppose the moral conscience and sensibility of both nations were educated up to such a pitch, would have no cause to be jealous of American territory, or French tactics, or German learning, or Cossack discipline. It seems to me Napoleon uttered a great fallacy, instead of a sage aphorism,—and just such a fallacy as the preponderance of the mere selfishly political over the moral perceptions might have prepared us to expect, — when he said, "America is a fortunate country, for she thrives by the follies of our European countries." No: folly in one nation does *not* help another.* It may set the balance of commercial exchange in her favor; it may pour into her lap a doubtful population; it may cast into her hands some temporary advantage, or leave her to a transient distinction. But it is the poor distinction that comes from having no honorable rivals. It is that sort of preëminence which is

* In 1642, the Earl of Bristol openly maintained, in the House of Lords, that it was a great advantage to England for other countries to be at war with each other, since by that means England would get possession of their wealth,—forgetting that in the long run wars are the destruction of wealth. See "Parliamentary History," vol. ii., page 1274. Since writing this passage, I have met with an able defence of the same doctrine in Buckle's "History of Civilization in England."

enjoyed in a class of dunces and sluggards by a boy who is only a little less a dunce and sluggard than the rest. It is the eminence of the stunted shrub on a sandy plain. Benefitted by other men's follies! Benefits have no such parentage. Only wisdom yields them, as only truth makes free.

We must acknowledge that the practical realization of these principles and these hopes in political institutions is slow. It is already nearly two thousand years since Cicero, Pagan prophet as he was, wrote these noble words: "There are those who deny that any bond of law or of association for purposes of common good exists among citizens. This opinion subverts all union in a State. There are those who deny that any such bond exists between themselves and strangers; and this opinion destroys the community of the human race." It is two centuries and a half since Lord Bacon, poor menial of a throne as his soaring and far-sighted intellect became, declared that there is in man's nature "a secret love of others, which, if not contracted, would expand and embrace all men." Yet how tardily does this sentiment,—this great "Law above all other laws, and Hope for Humanity," as Guizot pronounces it,—get itself recognized in the senates and cabinets, the overreaching diplomacy and the paltry palaces, of actual States! None the less is it every man's private obligation in his own place,—not less than that of statesmen and ministers of state and emperors,—to avow it, and stand by it, and be its consistent disciple. The day has broken into the sky. The shadow on the golden dial grows daily thinner, as the sun rises deliberately towards the eternal noon. Take the law of nations as an example. Nothing deserving that name had existence till these modern times. The barbarous tribes waited for it so long. Yet already the modifications and enlargements it has admitted indicate the progress of this spirit. From laws between nations we are evidently going on to duties between nations, and then to sympathies and courtesies. At first, the chief use was to secure treaties of traffic, and a public highway. But now the bonds are widening, and begin to embrace the great doctrine of Fraternity. America is eager to protect a victim of oppression, though he is hardly yet her own subject; and so diplomacy has to stretch its ancient precedents to accommodate this broader feeling of the age. It would be vain to expect any hasty completion of these ameliorations. But it is wise to mark their signals, and generous to hope for their fulfilment.

There have been systems in the world which denied all this,—systems specious and splendid,—some in ethics, some in political economy. But they have vanished like morning mists that lose and scatter themselves before the everlasting hills; or if they have lingered on, like those vapors they have had to settle and brood only in the low and less pure places where the mountain winds let decay alone. Take the system of Hobbes, denying the disinterested affections. Certainly it did not fail for want of gifts and powers in its defender. With a mind so acute and so original, blending so remarkably the usually separated capacities of discrimination and combination, as to make him the admiration of wits, the delight of scholars, and a model to philosophers, declared by Leibnitz one of the only two men of modern times capable of reducing morals and jurisprudence to a science, with a style which has been pronounced "the very perfection of didactic language," "knowing so well how to steer between pedantry and vulgarity that two centuries probably have not superannuated more than a dozen of his words," he has yet scarcely an avowed disciple to honor his name, scarcely a reader whom shame does not drive from his conclusions as from some crime revolting to humanity, certainly not an institution to extend or embody his principles. With him "a deliberate regard to personal interest is the only possible motive to human action. There is no sense of duty, no compunction at our own offences, no indignation against the crimes of others unless they affect our own safety, no secret cheerfulness shed over the heart by the practice of well-doing." Hence, mankind, with all their impulsive selfishness, must, in their cool and rational hours, reject and disdain his doctrine. His moral and political system, as another has well said, was "a palace of ice, transparent, exactly proportioned, majestic; but gradually undermined by the central warmth of human feeling, before it was thawed into muddy water by the sunshine of true philosophy." God, in his Almighty love, made mankind to love, help, serve, and bless one another. Thomas Hobbes, with his prudential selfishness, could not succeed.

It follows that every monopoly which erects private advantage against the general advantage,—observe, I do not say private advantage *in accordance with* the general advantage, but against it,—has God's providence for an antagonist. The great commercial schemes which propose to fatten and feast on poor men's poverty are toppled over; and bury their builders, or their builders' children under them.

> "The mills of God do slowly wind,
> But they at last to powder grind."

Servile insurrections, Sepoy mutinies, the years '89 and '48 in Paris, are only hints of this tremendous truth—as really as the miraculous night that killed the first-born of Egypt, and emancipated Israel. When the whole land of Italy came to be monopolized, as Gibbon says it was at one time, by seventeen hundred and sixty families,—only about as many as make up the city of Cincinnati,—no wonder the curse of a blighted population began to creep over the country. No class can put its interests forward at the expense of the rest. The selfish mob is just as false, just as inhuman, just as much the enemy of man and of true society, as the selfish monarch. "Open national workshops for us, and pay us your money," screeched the Parisian populace in 1848, "and we will down with the barricades." They had their way. *Socialism,* for the time, triumphed over *Society.* Suppose the experiment had gone on. These unemployed classes would have continued enriching themselves. They would have drawn money from the regular channels of trade, interrupted commerce, embarrassed capital, till employment would have ceased again. Society would have come round where it was before, to inequality, oppression, hunger, with the plague of anarchy and chaos thrown in. The empire supervened, and proved, perhaps, quite as significant an illustration of the principle, on less costly terms. Self-interest carried out to unscrupulous conclusions, and riding rough-shod over order, is, sooner or later, self-destruction; for it breaks up all those social ties and obligations without which man cannot be truly himself. No matter whether it appears in the genteel and legalized forms of corporate gluttony and insatiable financial aggrandizement, or in the savage starvation riots that prowl the streets when these bubbles burst, mocking and parodying the most pathetic appeals of human want—villains growling for "work and bread," who mean never to do a day's "work" if they can live by theft, and to eat every day something much spicier than "bread." The virtue of one class is the economy of all. The grasping avarice of one is the bankruptcy of all. Taxes—direct or indirect—for war, prisons, bad debts, carry up prices. Everything that sets man against his brother eats up the common substance. It hinders the law of mutual help. We call the axiom of Machiavelli, that the king is to rule for his own advantage, a monstrous and inhuman lie. But it is only one formal justification of that grasping temper which instigates man anywhere to live for himself alone—a temper as sternly reprobated by the inherent laws of the social nature as by Paul's thirteenth chapter to the Corinthians on charity.

If we had the life-time of Methuselah, we should all probably rejoice at last, not without a certain solemnity of thanksgiving, to see the quarrels of nations ending in their predestined reconciliations. The bitterest political antagonisms will grow friendly. Tariff and internal improvements, fishing-smack and mill-wheel, warehouse and market-garden, city and village, will form symmetrical features in a peaceful landscape. This heavenly estate on earth, the last triumph of social economy in the great family mansion of our life,—the true golden age of the Future,—it is for Christianity alone to achieve; solving the hardest problems of our social state, and covering the earth with righteous institutions. Then national policy will be, not repulsion, but attraction; or rather policy will cease, and principle be installed. The game called politics,—that crafty match of mutual hindrance,—will give place to a benignant science of mutual helps,—where governments are only branches in an associate moral organism. The State will legislate order, justice, liberty. The school will teach truth. The church will live and pray like the Christ.

To further the final inauguration of that royal social age, every nation that has flourished under the sun has been ordained by the Creator and Father of them all. Each has brought in its hand, or its head, or its heart, some necessary contribution. And then the races shall meet together and dwell in peace; the strong heart of the Saxon, without his bloody hand; the graceful, courtly Norman, without his levity and pride; the brave Celt, without his impudent ferocity; the vigorous, iron-willed "Senatus Populusque Romanus," without the audacity and cruelty of its eagles; Egypt, meditative, but cleared of its mysticism; Greece, ingenious, beautiful, aspiring, redeemed from its idolatry of Beauty to the worship of God; the Hebrew, with his reverent ritual, but without his national hatred and suspicion; Chaldea and Shinar, forgetting even their lofty superstitions and looking above the stars to Him that holdeth them in his right hand; and all adoring the invisible Father acceptably, because they come to the altar reconciled to the brother whom they have seen. For, whether there be tongues, they shall cease; and, whether there be knowledge, it shall vanish away. But faith and hope and charity abide; and the greatest, still, is charity.

LECTURE V.

SOCIAL THEORIES.

We had reached, towards the close of the last lecture, a distinction between Social Science and Socialism. Uneasy at the inequalities, the false distinctions, the miseries, which he sees prevailing in the world around him, or perhaps feels pressing upon him, the Socialist refers them to particular social conditions and circumstances. Society, and human nature in all states of Society, are confounded; and the evils that spring from the latter are ascribed to the former. By a logical inversion, it is proposed to cure the disordered cause through the effect, not the effect through the cause.

In order to strike the principle which must guide our present discussion, we have to recall that great twofold law of man's constitution which sets him in equipoise between the claims and ministries of associate life, on the one side, and his own individuality on the other.

Nature has two purposes with him—first, to make the most of him as a unit, by developing all the personal quality and personal force peculiar to himself; and second, to turn him to the best account, in the way of reception and action, as an educated and living influence among his fellows. There is an error on two sides, and a loss from both, in the violation of this design of the Creator. Society, as a system of mutual dependencies and assistances, may be sacrificed to the individual, as by Hobbes. The individual may be sacrificed to Society; this is Socialism, which stands in much the same relation to Society, as conventionalism to good manners, artifice to art, sciolism to science, or pietism to piety.

Each mistake may spring from a selfish spirit, or not. Contemplating, as we have now to do, the socialist theories, and seeing how often they have had their origin in a sincere desire to benefit the less favored classes, or in a reaction from real injustice and frightful abuses of wealth and position, we can well afford to treat them with respect. Nay, as we would seek to displace them, we cannot afford to treat them otherwise, however popular it may have been to attack them with ridicule or contempt. I believe that a fair inquiry into their purport, arguments, and operation, will result, by contrast, in the confirmation of our principal proposition, that Society in itself is an illustration of the Power, and Wisdom, and Goodness of God.

Socialism has frequently been assailed, on the ground that its systems for arranging mankind are artificial, while Nature is the only safe guide. With suitable discriminations and definitions, there is validity in this objection. But we must take care what we mean by Nature, and what others understand us to mean. For in our human nature there are terrible forces of evil, as well as powers of light and love. Besides, although the socialist theories look artificial to their opponents, we must remember that it is claimed for them by their several advocates that they are a simple and happy way of returning to Nature, and of giving the providential laws a freer play. On the whole, it appears to me, that when our reason, our political economy, our philosophy, and our prejudices, have all uttered their protest, and passed their criticism, the only really effectual refutation of these errors, after all, must be drawn from one of two sources: the lessons of historical experience, and the gospel of Christ. Of these two, the first alone will not be adequate: for new exigencies are liable to arise continually, for which the precedents of the past provide no perfect rule. The teachings of Christianity alone are infallible and final. And so long as of those a divine sacrifice is the central fact, the cross is the universal symbol, and self-denial the characteristic spirit and essential duty, so long the systems that aim chiefly to make life easy and to free it from care, and to accommodate it to self-will, must be adjudged false and futile. It is, at least, a conflict, in which one party or the other must be utterly overthrown.

The grand aim of all those schemes known under both the names of Socialism and Communism, has been to regulate, by external arrangement, the three great interests, Labor, Property, and the Passions, and especially the passion of sex. At the root of all these schemes has been that idea of human equality of which Rousseau was the leading apostle. It is undoubtedly owing either to the influence of that man on the modern French mind, or else to a national characteristic of which he was a remarkable exponent, that France has been the principal theatre of these socialist experiments. Strictly speaking, the attempt to secure the proposed equality by means of labor is Socialism; the attempt to secure it by means of the abolition of property is Communism.

Without, at this moment, referring to all the specific varieties of theory, we may say that with respect to Labor, the object has been to produce a greater equality, a smaller amount, — relatively to the production of value,—and more willingness, or agreeableness, in the performance. Under each of these proposals we can detect its own distinct and particular fallacy. First: the Socialist, instead of producing equality of labor, is so to distribute the work that every man and woman shall have just that work to do which each can do best, and which each will therefore choose. But it is by no means a uniform rule that men choose to do the work that they are best fitted for, nor that they are capable of telling what their real adaptations are, nor that anybody can tell without that sort of experimenting and comparison which take place in the ordinary social competition.

So of private Property: the allegation is that the acquisition of it, by the existing competitory methods, stimulates selfish and alienating propensities; that its inequalities lead to other moral evils and abuses; and that wealth produces a dangerous and oppressive kind of power. To which it is replied, 1. That the stimulus of personal thrift develops energies, also, which are a positive good. 2. That the very temptations to fraud and to excess, in avarice, covetousness and luxury, which attend the present system of competition, form a necessary and providential school for virtue, offering a discipline without which it would never acquire its due robustness and independence; and 3. That, in the same way, over against the abuses of riches are set those possible advantages of personal beneficence, public spirit, and wise expenditure, which furnish a nobler exercise to humanity than a monotonous, inevitable, involuntary comfort:—besides which is urged the impossibility of equalizing the conditions of men, whose natural capacities are made unequal by their Creator, however often you throw into common stock and re-distribute their goods.

Of the Passions, whereas it is affirmed by Socialism that their evils spring from the resistances they meet, philosophy answers, No; but from their own excesses. Whereas Socialism says they are to be managed through outward circumstances, experience says, No; but by an inward principle in every soul, which is equal to their mastery; and whereas Socialism teaches that the conflicts of the desires are to cease by their indulgence, Christianity teaches that they can be controlled only by their subjection to conscience, and their submission to the law of God. "Without piety," says the terse and thoughtful author of "Friends in Council," "there will be no good government."

Observe here, that something of the socialist spirit and sophistry attach to those measures of special combination which, without collecting communities of people, and often with the kindest intention, do virtually interfere with what may be called, without begging the question, the regular action of the social Family, and break in upon the mutual understanding, and the implied good faith ot different branches of industry in the hands of individuals.

Leagues among working classes, for cheapening provisions, disturb the common balance and broad partnership of the employments, by a class privilege, and are just as contrary to a true social spirit as the class privileges of aristocratic wealth. The English Trades' Unions, which proposed to do away with the master mechanics, failed. So did Mr. Babbage's proposed scheme of association, for reducing the cost of the necessaries of life among factory operatives. Sumptuary legislation, or legislation that undertakes to coerce private morality, or to force the free relations of capital and labor, comes to the same unfortunate end. By an act of Parliament of 1773, a rule of minimum wages, *i. e.*, a rule providing that wages should never go below a certain point, was applied to the Spitalfields weavers. It was intended to protect the interests of the operatives; but in twenty years four thousand looms were standing idle, and the hands were out of work and wages both. Strikes among workmen illustrate the same suicidal policy of attempting to compel one class to conform to the will of another, and to take the course of demand and supply in employment out of its natural channels. Labor depends on capital. Strikes diminish the capital by suspending the work. Of course they diminish, the further they go, the means of raising wages, and defeat their own object. It is the industry of the working classes that increases the prosperity of the employer, and thus the workman's own wages. Each helps the other. In seasons of pressure, when the markets are dull, and goods too plenty, the manufacturing company are obliged to contract their operations. If the operatives will take up, temporarily, with reduced pay, both survive, though both suffer. But if the operatives refuse, then the mills stop, and all alike may be crushed.

The recognition of those laws of reciprocal harmony and interdependence, which bind the several trades and professions together, is a matter of profound importance, not only to our philosophy of Reform, but to our personal conduct, especially in periods of financial distress, and our general practical applications of the principles of political economy. It explodes if it does not silence much of the fallacious and illogical exhortation which springs to the lips of superficial moralists, in "Hard Times," about retrenchment in expenditure. Precisely because the different employments of Society do thus depend on each other, the duty of wise men, when any of them are embarrassed, is to keep the rate of expenditure as nearly as possible at its usual average amount. The disorder is a depressed state of credit and currency. If now your classes that are really able and competent to buy, suddenly change their whole habit, hearken to this indiscriminate cry for retrenchment, and cut off all the comforts and luxuries they can possibly spare, what is the necessary effect? They stop the currents of small trade, — those rills that feed ten thousand homes, disappoint the traders, throw an unsaleable stock upon their hands, bring down calamity from the great establishments and manufacturing corporations into the retail department, and turn these industrious tradesmen, mechanics, florists, dress-makers, servants, into paupers. Could a policy be devised more exactly calculated to aggravate the disease and increase the confusion? Some branches of business deal wholly in those fanciful and ornamental articles which, in moments of alarm, or real loss, people first pronounce superfluous. Doubtless, individual judgment must be applied to particular cases. Men who have not money to spend cannot spend it. There is a line between liberality and extravagance. But nothing ought to be plainer than that abrupt alterations in modes of living are a wrong inflicted by one class on another, violating the gracious principle of their mutual dependence. To all persons whose means are not actually stripped away, that law says, "Postpone your reductions for the present; economize by and bye; use discretion always; go not beyond your means; incur no rash debts; but, otherwise, as to the comforts and even the luxuries in which you have been accustomed to indulge, preserve as nearly as possible the ordinary rule of outlay, and so satisfy the commercial expectations which your past habits have reasonably awakened. Shocks and convulsions are the malady; cure them, so far as lies in your power, by a regular and uniform disbursement."

I pass on now to some description and some criticism of different theories of Socialism. We have to distinguish, at the outset, between the more elaborate and ambitious forms of socialist speculation, and certain local communities, gathered on an exceptional basis, for particular objects. Such as these latter are the various religious communities that have been organized, in different periods, by the spirit of asceticism, or charity, or a separating enthusiasm, or a purity repelled from surrounding falsehood and corruption. It can scarcely be pretended that the monks, the Moravians, the Jesuits of Paraguay, the Shakers, even when their societies were most flourishing, contemplated a complete social plan. They did not profess to meet all social wants. Religious faith and zeal commonly protected them from many of the worst mischiefs, though we cannot help regarding even them as deviations from a true social economy. The sexes were separated. Everything bore the character of an exceptional and temporary provision. This was emphatically true of the very incidental and limited communistic element in the Apostolic church. And though the Christian monasticism of the following centuries was far more systematic and presumptuous, yet, in its wildest fanaticism, it never pretended to be a universal social scheme.

Some of the elements of Communism were introduced into the ancient State of Lacedæmon. Plutarch, in his Life of Lycurgus, gives an account of the attempts of that legislator to throw the landed property of the nation into common stock, and then to equalize it. The project originated, apparently, in a benevolent purpose; but it resulted in a miserable despotism. The Spartan had no household, no home. If allowed to marry at all, his married life was still subject to public supervision. The State watched and controlled him; and what the State wanted was to breed warriors. If the sight of their children made fathers too tender-hearted for that, they must either not beget children, or not live with them, or even refuse to see them. Among the free citizens there must be no commerce, no dealings in money. All traffic and artizanship were handed over to the helots. It was a tremendous piece of coercion; a strange mixture of Socialism and tyranny,—a model not likely to find copies.

Socialist reformers sometimes refer to the authority of Plato. Plato's political system was invented as a kind of practical illustration of his whole ethical and metaphysical philosophy. The Dialogue on the Republic, where this system is unfolded, is a summary, or rather a logical terminus, of all his ideas of being, morality, general science, and civil organization. It opens with an abstract discussion of the nature of Justice, and passes out into an ideal representation of the embodiment of Right in a city or a State. The State is considered as an exhibition (παραδειγμα) of the individual. Yet "the State takes its rise because none of us individually happens to be self-sufficient." Plato divides the citizens of his ideal republic into three classes, the deliberative, the auxiliary, and the money-making. The administration of the government, for peace and war, should be committed to the highest, that is, the wisest, purest, best bred order of men and women,—whom he calls the philosophers. These guardians should have their training at the public cost and should be without property, so as to be exempt from all the calculations, anxieties and sordid overreachings which corrupt and distract a ruler's mind. To release them more effectually from domestic care and ambition, the family should be abolished, and a community of wives and children take its place. The two grand departments of education should be music and gymnastics,—which may perhaps better be rendered, the harmonious development and the vigorous discipline of the powers. Poetry should be, for the most part, excluded, partly because it tends to the enervation and relaxing of the stronger forces of the soul, and partly for the subtle reason that, as all things may be said, in the Platonic scheme, to exist originally in the idea, or invisible form, and secondly, to be produced in a sensible shape, the poet, who only pictures this sensible shape, really gives us the thing at the third remove from the original fact. Thus a common table exists first in its archetypal idea; secondly, in the wooden shape of legs and leaves formed by the cabinet-maker; and thirdly, in the illusive representation or description of a poet or an artist. The work of this latter, being imitative in the second degree, is superfluous and useless. In every respect, Plato aims at real advantages, the most complete subjugation of the passions, and an elevated heathen morality.

Of the different kinds of government he designates five. The first is that which he recommends as accordant with Right, the true welfare of a commonwealth. This is an aristocracy; only the word is taken not in its present popular sense, but literally, as denoting a government of those persons from the people who are everyway best,—most competent, brave, patriotic, learned, and disinterested. Contrasted with this are four faulty kinds of rule: a timocracy, or government of ambition; an oligarchy; a democracy; and a despotism.

In its lofty requirement of self-denial, this Platonic Socialism differs totally from the modern theories. *Nor is the view carried out into all their* minuteness of detail. With its many defects and mistakes, it is incapable of mischief, hanging there in the cool, rare atmosphere of intellectual speculation,—a city in the air. Plato's own language at the outset is, "as if we were talking in the way of fable."* Yet the Dialogue is one of the masterpieces of the most imperial mind of antiquity, and is a sublime illustration of the great Platonic idea, that Good is a social principle. In this it exhibits that singular combination of dialectic force with humane designs which has always struck Plato's interpreters as wonderful, and which led one of them to say, "Plato's great object was man. He lived with man, felt as a man, held intercourse with kings, interested himself deeply in the political revolutions of Sicily, was the pupil of one whose boast it was to have brought down philosophy from heaven to earth that it might raise man up from earth to heaven; and, above all, he was a witness and an actor in the midst of that ferment of humanity exhibited in the democracy of Athens."

Of the Utopias, the two most remarkable, perhaps, are those of Sir Thomas More and James Harrington. More wrote the work which gives a name to the whole class, while he was receiving the most dazzling attentions from his sovereign, and was really the most signal person of his age in England. It was about the year 1518 that it was published, in Latin, at Basle. From his early youth, this great political genius and incorruptible

* Book ii., chapter 17.

patriot had been a student of civil institutions, public law, and forensic eloquence. Neither the court nor the times favored a virtue so rare. The great thinker used to steal away from the festivities and garden walks where the king fondled and flattered him, to write out his dream of a happy commonwealth. Imagining an island, of lovely scenery and delightful climate, in the western seas, he peoples it with the virtuous, prosperous groups. The name, Utopia, is taken from that of a supposed hero, or leader, Utopus. The work is an extended description of the laws, customs, religion, occupations, of this imaginary settlement, including some communistic features. The mixture of what is grotesque and frivolous with what is noble and true, has puzzled many of the commentators. The probable key to the plan is furnished by the theory that More wished to publish views of government and society very dear to himself, but more liberal and enlightened than Henry VIII. or his age would tolerate, if they were put forth in a serious form and by a direct argument. Resorting to a device of fancy, therefore, and intermingling much which should carry its own explanation as merely a fantastic or chimerical entertainment, the sagacious statesman yet contrived to introduce and to commend some of his noblest doctrines of freedom, conscience, and a lofty standard of political ethics. This comports with the spirit of the earnest martyr to the simple conviction of Right, who not long after gave his head to the axe rather than connive at the domestic crimes of his king. But there is nothing to indicate that More was drawing out a definite pattern of any social system to be realized among men.

James Harrington was a contemporary of the first settlers of New England. Though an Oxford scholar, and an officer in the royal household of Charles I., he was a stanch republican, and was at last driven to side with the Roundheads. His "Oceana," published in 1656, was a political romance,—its fictitious form being adopted as a convenient vehicle for the author's passionate attachment to the principles of freedom. As the plan of a State, it has exerted no force; and with all its literary merit, it has probably been much less read than the "Utopia" of More.

The great name in modern Socialism is Charles Fourier. Fourier is entitled to this preëminence on several accounts: by the boldness and thoroughness of his theory; by the minute, systematic, and, we may even say, the formally scientific arrangement and distribution of all the parts of his plan; by the intellectual brilliancy and eloquent audacity with which he thrust his stupendous absurdity upon the incredulity, and yet conquered for it the admiration, of the thinking world; and by the strange, the almost whimsical contrast between the splendor of the imaginary scenes he pictured for the future of our race and the narrow and dingy accompaniments of his own personal condition.

This French visionary, who might have been a philosopher if philosophy were never subjected to the test of practice, or who might have been a poet if he had not indulged in imaginations meant to be put into practical operation, was the son of a cloth dealer, and was born eighty-six years ago, at Besançon, in France. His entire life he spent in subordinate situations in mercantile establishments, at Marseilles, Lyons and Paris, and most of it in obscurity and poverty. Amidst this routine of drudgery and this contracted scenery, there passed before him the gorgeous spectacle of a renovated earth, a reconstructed Humanity, a social state glorious as any ideal conception of Paradise itself. Nor was it in his conception, apparently, altogether a cloudy, confused vision, all a dream to him, and all rhetoric to his reader. Rigorous and exact rules of the mathematics were applied to it. It was a careful and complicated compound of morals, fancies, principles and numbers. The arithmetic proportion of his phalansteries was based on the calculations of Newton. And there is scarcely a department of human knowledge with which the learning of his voluminous works does not, in some way, intermeddle.

For the publication of his compositions, which he commenced in 1808, he depended on the assistance of some wealthy friends.* The first few disciples that could be prevailed on to read these extravagant writings, and were credulous enough to yield to them, were not found till he was more than fifty years old, about 1825. The French revolution of five years later unsettled the old order, and opened the ear of public fanaticism and discontent to any imposing vagary that promised ease, comfort, enjoyment, with little labor, less self-restraint and no sacrifice. It proved, however, that, both then and in the still more favorable disorganizations of 1848, insuperable obstacles existed to the popularizing of his works. Such as were published found able expositors, defenders, and translators, in his own country, in England, and even in America. These digests and interpretations, however, no matter

* The most important of these to the student of his system are entitled "*Traitè d'Association Domestique Agricole*," "*Théorie des Quatres Mouvements et des Destinées Générales*," and "*Le Nouveau Monde Industriel et Societaire.*"

how warm the spirit of championship in which they were conceived, gave him little comfort. He always maintained, even to the close of his disappointed life, and with pretty good reason, that nobody understood his ideas, and that no representation whatever, but his own, could be fairly made of his doctrines; and to this day, his most impartial and competent readers are left in doubt whether it can be said that even his own representation is more successful than the rest. Some slight but fatal defect, enough to mar the unity of the whole, clung to the ardent attempts of his best instructed advocates. Indeed, the greater part of his immense mass of manuscript remains unpublished still, in the Phalansterian Academy at Paris.

Such a state of being as an indolent and pleasure-loving community would delight in was certainly promised by this prophet after their own heart. Nothing could have prevented their hailing and crowning him as the universal Deliverer, except the serious inconvenience of being unable to believe what he said. His golden age was to be the fulfilment of every sensual desire,—the complete, unhindered, if not inexhaustible gratification of every passion of human nature; and these gratifications were to be constantly, in every instance, as intense and ecstatic as the keenest relish of our rarest bliss hitherto.* It must be added, that the joys of the intellect and the heart were to be in proportion, and also that he held the passions to be sacred, as the gift of God. So perfectly, in the new order, would mind and body and affections be trained, balanced and preserved, — so marvellously would nature yield up her stores of nutriment and energy, that humanity would be rejuvenated,—all sweat and care and toil and disappointment would cease, and the most necessary offices, such as are now irksome and homely, would be as fresh and inviting as the most exhilarating sports. If this grand carnival of unsatiated appetites required so great an innovation on the part of Nature as the production of a new species of animals, Fourier would not stick at that. Who was he, to stint her prodigality, or distrust the accommodating possibilities of her bounty ? What was a new natural element or two, in view of a result so magnificent ? To accomplish a more rapid transit to and fro, and convey the pleasant

* " M. Fourier boasts to have made the grand discovery that our varied passions, if left to themselves, would so counteract, so supplement each other, that the most complete harmony would result. If so, how happens it that Society did not at once arrange itself into this perfect harmony by the spontaneous passions of men ? Spontaneity comes before reflection. How is it that human society was not at once complete, like the society of bees and of ants ?"—THORNDALE.

provisions of one climate to another, unprecedented tame creatures, of the lion and the whale kind, swift and capacious, were to make their appearance, as transcendental beasts of burden. The planets themselves were to procreate their own species, and to furnish each other their respective types of existence, in amicable interchange. The mineral, vegetable and animal kingdoms of our globe receive contributions from all the moons and orbs of the solar system; the elephant, the oak, and the diamond being created by the sun himself,—the horse, the lily and the ruby by Saturn,—the cow, the jonquil and the topaz by Jupiter,—the dog, the violet and opal stones by the Earth.

Starting with the complaint that Society in its present competitive condition is a "universal state of war," Fourier claimed to have discovered the secret of its restoration to harmony. The key to the universe is the "law of attraction." In the grand whole of nature there are four "movements," in an ascending scale, viz., the material, the organic, the animal, the social. To these he afterward added a fifth, the aromal, which is to be the consummation of all perfect order and joy, corresponding to the Christian millennium. Even previous to this aromal stage, marvellous ameliorations and novelties are to appear. So ecstatic and transcendant, in fact, will be the felicities of that period, produced by the new social organization, that great precaution is necessary in announcing them to mankind, lest a too sudden disclosure should bewitch the world into a general delirium. The Prophet reveals only a few features of that ineffable glory. The word toil will lose its meaning. Work will be play, and play will be more productive of solid use than work was ever known to be. Slavery will cease. Woman will be elevated out of all her disabilities. The duration of man's life will be a hundred and forty years. His period of love will be a hundred and twenty years. Changes in the material world will correspond to those in the moral. The Arctic climate will soften. The ocean will be sweet. Four moons will accompany the earth, which is the third planet. Death will introduce man to the aromal life. And when the course of the world itself is finished, the earth-life will be handed over to the planet Mercury.

The chief agent of this social regeneration was to be the phalange, or phalanstery; or rather, the perpetual society of man must exist in that form, —a series of groups. Each of these was to consist of four hundred families, averaging four and a half persons each, making eighteen hundred in all. The word family is not used here in the ordinary sense; the family founded in marriage, consisting of parents and children, is an evil to be got rid of. The financial value was to be held in eleven hundred and twenty-eight shares, determined by a very nice mathematical computation; and of these shares five twelfths were to accrue to labor, four twelfths to capital, and three twelfths to skill. Ultimately the whole world was to be covered with phalanges. All necessities were to be provided by them, but commercial interchange was not recognized. The head of all the phalanges was to be an omniarch, located at Constantinople. Each group was to be composed according to passional attractions and affinities. As there is harmony between every passion and its object, so there is harmony between the passions and all necessary labor. Some kind of work is pleasant to all. Some children love dirt; this shows that there are some people made for dirty employment. All the passions of which human nature is capable will be represented by sixteen hundred and twenty persons, rightly chosen. Consult the proper adaptations, and all the productive industries would be carried forward, while mankind should not suspect they were doing anything but amuse themselves. Everybody should be able to do only what he pleases, meet only people that are agreeable, eat only what he likes, obey nothing but his propensities. No discord; no offence; no crosses; no fatigue; no unsatisfied want; no indigestion; no plague, or pain, or fear, or tediousness, from social collisions, or lack of sympathy. Of course morality is quite dissolved, or superseded. Constancy is forgotten. The offset to this is, that, in this higher condition, the passions are purified; they do not chafe nor surfeit; the appetites lose their grossness; and there is no sin.

Fourier held that his system of the social economy would come, historically, next after Christianity, advancing beyond that, and would be the third grand dispensation. Hitherto, he taught, man is in a state only of civilization—*civilizée*. Now, civilization is only the fifth of thirty-two possible states of Society; the rest are to come. Civilization is for the rich, who are only a twentieth part of the race. Its principle is the "war of all against all." Competition is anarchy. Property is an evil. In rejecting civilization the instincts of savages and barbarians are right. The only relief to its greediness is self-denial, which, after all, is another principal misery. From civilization the transition into the harmonial society will not be less remarkable than the metamorphosis of the worm into the butterfly. "The passions and their gratifications will be so multiplied by each other as to produce square or cubical quantities of felicity, rational and several,—without frailty or reaction." In following out this conception, Fourier was led into exposures of unhealthy and unreasonable modes of living, the neglect and filth and inconvenience of great cities especially, and other errors in the economic and industrial habits of different nations, which have a real sanitary value, and are adapted to prepare the way for reforms more practicable than he proposed. Indeed, the term practicability can scarcely be used in connection with his splendid ideal fabric, except in irony. It has been justly said that the one formidable enemy he had to meet was the putting of his own theory to experiment: though it was curious that he, by a secret prognostication wiser than his brain, expected it would fail. A phalanx was started at Rambouillet, not far from Paris. The cost of the fruitless trial was estimated at £20,000. The fate of the little undertakings suggested by him in our own neighborhood is too well known to need remark. Notwithstanding, Fourier seems to have been a bigot for his own notions, to the last. Six years before his death, which happened in 1837, he wrote a severe and bitter treatise against the follies and impostures of two speculators everyway as sound as himself, and called it, *The Tricks and Charlatanry of two Sects, St. Simon and Owen.**

Claude Henry, St. Simon, was twelve years older than Fourier, and died just twelve years before him. He was of a very different social position from his fellow-countryman, was born of an aristocratic family, descended from noble blood, indeed claiming descent from Charlemagne. The best account of him is that he was properly a victim of scientific ambition. Whether as the cause or the effect of that ambition, he appears to have fostered a foolish rumor that his royal ancestor appeared to him in a dream and told him that their house, having produced a great monarch, was destined to produce a great philosopher. Acting on this nocturnal hint, the young scion of the old noblesse united his resources as a gentleman and a student to earn the reputation he coveted. He took a residence near the Polytechnic School and threw open his private hospitalities to a series of brilliant meetings of the savans and forcible men of his time,—reserving to himself the high office of generalizer and judge upon the results of their investigations. When Napoleon proposed to the Institute to make a formal estimate of the achievements of science, St. Simon undertook to conduct

* "Piéges et Charlatanisme des deux Sectes,—St. Simon et Owen."

the answer. His travels and extensive researches were all made to bear on his philosophical fame. Even when he was a youthful soldier in the cavalry service, taking a hint from Philip, with a variation, he kept up the flattery of a great destiny by bidding his servant call him every morning: "Awake, Sir Count, you have great things to do."* He impoverished himself in his ostentatious and luxurious patronage of letters, and then made light of his penury, as an interesting phase of human experience, which it became a philosopher, like him, to pass through. Carrying out this idea, he committed himself, in succession, not only to all the other situations of life, but to the unprincipled practice of the whole catalogue of vices,—as a simple experiment in physics and ethics. Even suicide was included in this list of amateur manipulations, though for some reason or other he carried that only so far as to blow out one of his eyes. With extravagant and profane laudations his admirers celebrated this escape. "His hour," they said, "was not yet come. God raises him from the abyss; sheds over him a religious inspiration which animates, sanctifies and renews his whole being; a hymn of love is poured forth from that

* "Levez-vous, Monsieur le Comte, vous avez de grandes choses à faire."

mutilated body; the divine man is manifested; the new Christianity is sent to the world; the kingdom of God is come upon earth."

The St. Simonian Socialism was an attempt to carry out the definite and regular relations of physical science into the government or rather the arrangement of Society; which it was believed, by a false analogy, could be done with abstract certainty, by rule. The author of the system called it "Physico-political." Property, competition, marriage, were to be summarily abolished. Inclination was to govern. Christianity was caricatured. The system was a "carnal hierarchy,"—the proposed leaders were a priesthood. The originator was himself, during life, and after that his foremost disciple, to be the great hierophant. In fact, he claimed the character of divinity,—profanely ranking himself with Moses and the Saviour, saying that "Moses had promised to men universal fraternity, Jesus Christ had prepared it, St. Simon had realized it."

Mutual and natural human love is here made the organizing principle. Industry is the working power of life. "Sanctify yourselves by joy and labor," says the new Christianism. This ("New Christianism") is the title of his religious speculations. Other parts of his system were published under the titles of "The Reorganization of European Society," "The Industrial System," "Catechism of Industrial Methods," "Political, Moral, and Philosophical Discussions," and "Opinions."

According to this form of Socialism, the distribution of property was to be determined by the relative capacity of men; whereas, according to Fourier, capacity had to divide with labor and capital. At the death of an individual his property reverts to the Simonian community—the secular church. A general education was to be provided for all children till they were old enough to show their capacity, and then *chacun à sa capacité*.

About a quarter of a century since, there emerged from the confused and motley people known as St. Simonians three several parties, under as many leaders—Enfantin, Rodriguez, and Basard. Each attempted his own organizations, or families, but they quarreled with each other. At last the two former were brought to trial for misdemeanors, and underwent a temporary punishment. Enfantin appeared in the streets of Paris, and pointing to his handsome face, demanded homage on the score of his personal beauty. When some of the leaders applied for exemption from military duty, on the impudent pretence that they were ecclesiastics, the courts ruled that they were not a religious order.

but otherwise let their extravagances and sensual carousals pass unnoticed, till finally the whole scheme fell to pieces, and disappeared.

These projects have not been confined to France. They have struck root, for a short and sickly growth, in practical Great Britain and America. The same year that Fourier was born brought also his English competitor,—a Socialist whose scheme was far less daring, less presumptuous, and less visionary than that of the Frenchman who so violently assailed it for its absurdity. Robert Owen became a cotton-machinist at Manchester, and afterwards entered upon the manufacturing experiment at New Lanark, on the Clyde, in Scotland, which proved an interesting comment upon his theories. Actuated by a sincere and humane desire to better the condition of the dependent and laboring classes, especially in the peculiar exposures incident to British manufacturing towns, he undertook so to arrange that whole community, as to lighten their expenses and increase their conveniences. Noticing how much the application of superior energy and intelligence, in improving the circumstances of a people, assists their culture and development, he was fallaciously led to suppose that all human reform must consist in changing these external circumstances, and so, from a peculiar instance, fell into a false generalization. Because one shrewd and active manager like himself, having capital to start with, in a special branch of productive industry, already brought elsewhere to great perfection, could organize a successful local settlement, keeping up a constant commerce with Society in its normal forms, and under a stable government, he seems to have supposed that all populations must contain in them the means of first rising above and so ruling their own conditions, with mixed employments, complicated interests, and a thousand other specific modifying causes. A town is laid out in the form of a parallelogram, with buildings for two or three thousand souls, with gardens and farms and agricultural edifices on each side, land enough to furnish all the necessary produce of that climate,—the dwelling houses forming one side of the oblong square, a general residence and schools for the boys at one end, similar provisions for the girls at the other end,—the children being taken from their parents and boarded together in their second year, a common eating-house or ordinary in the centre, play grounds and gardens in the area, laundry and bleaching grounds behind the school houses. There is a suitable alternation of labor and recreation. The working hours are from six in the morning to seven in the evening. The school is held from eight in the evening till ten. Amusements are provided by system, as being favorable to morality. The community of goods is only partial, but the plan of industrial coöperation is distinct.

Whatever Mr. Owen may have borrowed from the Moravians, or United Brethren, it is very clear what he left out, viz., their religion. With him a happy and correct social state here is the ultimate object of man's aspirations. All systems of faith and worship he refers to prejudice, superstition and ignorance. The sanctions of a future life are set aside as not only chimerical but mischievous. Christianity is superseded.

Carried away by the prosperity of his village at New Lanark, which, after all, appears to have been due about as much to the practical sagacity and benevolence of his predecessor and father-in-law, David Dale, as to his own theory, which ought certainly to be tested by a trial of more than one or two generations before a strong argument can be built upon it,—this amiable unbeliever supposed he had struck upon a universal cure for social evils. To prove this on a larger scale, he began a parallelogram at Orbiston; but the design fell through for want of funds, after one angle of the structure was erected. The inmates of this angle, while they stayed, were not lovely and pleasant in their lives; the country people called the place Babel, for reasons. In 1825 he purchased the place known as New Harmony, in Indiana, planted a colony of nearly a thousand people, turned the churches into workshops, substituted singing and dancing for public prayer, proclaimed marriage a temporary, dissoluble relation, removed the obstacle to a separation of husband and wife that exists in the children by putting them into a common charge, published a Declaration of Mental Independence, July 4th, 1826, but soon found he had to manage discontent and disorder, was disgusted, and returned across the ocean, escaping from a broken-down enterprise.*

The neighboring State of Illinois was to see, still nearer to our own time, another of these abortive undertakings, — that conducted by Cabet, another creature of the modern revolutionary spirit in France. To carry out his preposterous project, a compound of financial and political speculation, this plausible adventurer, in whom it is difficult to draw the line between honest self-delusion and villainous imposture, gave out that he had bought a million

* See his "Observations on the Manufacturing System," "New View of Society," and "Memorial to the Governments of England and America."

acres of American land, at Icaria, on the Red River. There he proposed to plant a community, on the socialist plan, holding out the promise of a luxuriant soil, delightful scenery, and everything favorable to an easy mastery of the means of living. By a newspaper, called *La Populaire,* and other devices, he succeeded in alluring some five hundred emigrants to embark, in 1848, for this gorgeous western Paradise, — having first gained assent to the incredible regulation that all their individual property should be unconditionally committed to their leader, himself, — a stupendous stretch of communistic confidence. Landing at New Orleans, they met rather appalling accounts of the Icarian Eden from some returning pioneers, but still pressed hopefully up the Mississippi; traversed a land route of two or three hundred miles, —many perishing by the way, some dropping out of the party and going back, fleeced and dejected, to their native country,—the persevering survivors arriving at last at the promised land, to find there, in the expressive language of the record, "a desert, a few ruined huts, and an abundance of graves." "There is no slavery," wrote one of them, "so hard as Communism in action."* In a

* "*Les Socialistes depuis Fourier.*" Par M. Jules Breynat. Paris, 1850.

short time, Cabet, gathering up as many of the fragments of resolution and baggage as he could find, left, passed up to Nauvoo, then recently vacated by the Mormons on their removal to Utah, and there remained just long enough to fail utterly, and to subject himself to a criminal prosecution, on the charge of obtaining goods on false pretences.

In 1840, a petition was sent to the British House of Lords, with forty thousand signers from the single city of Birmingham, praying that measures might be taken for the suppression of Socialism. Nothing effectual was done by Parliament; indeed, a brief reaction took place in favor of the Socialists. But it soon subsided; the publications ceased; and the cause in all England died out.

These repeated miscarriages of Communism, regarded in the light of the moral principles of Society, are not surprising; and yet, considering the tact and ability of some of the projecters of these systems, the credulous constitution of human nature as respects schemes of pecuniary profit, and the natural effect of glowing descriptions of a leisurely and novel mode of subsistence, there is room for some surprise that their victims should have been so few, and their fate so uniform, so prompt, and so decisive. In 1848 a flood of communistic literature broke loose over Europe, and for a while was thirstily drunk up, especially in Germany and France. Now, there is scarcely such a literature visible, outside of the libraries, on the Continent.

Of the three contemporary authors who are best known as Socialists in their philosophy, though without heading any actual communities, the first, in point of intellectual power, is Auguste Comte,— a writer who by his frigid temperament, his unsympathetic doctrines of man, and his atheism, not less than by his arrogant erudition, is separated from popular interests, and exerts but a feeble influence on his own age. His system of Positive Philosophy, so far as it can be defined in a sentence, teaches that every possible department of thought and action is finally to be brought into the domain of the exact and fixed sciences by the domination of the understanding; that the cosmical order of creation forbids the supposition of a Personal Creative Will, or a God; and that the last of the sciences to be positively perfected will be Sociology, under which all men will have their positions of higher and lower, advantage and subordination, absolutely determined as by a decree of fate, under a rule, not to say a tyranny, of the strongest heads. He expects entire acquiescence in this arrangement. As this is to be the final achievement of perfected science, of course the realization of his ideal of social harmony is postponed to an extremely distant future.

Proudhon and Louis Blanc both aim at the virtual destruction of property; the former in the spirit of a destructionist, the latter in that of political ambition. Proudhon would level, at once, all distinctions of wealth, throw the world's value into a common fund, and let individuals draw out, not indeed by a general scramble, but by the definite proportion of each one's service. Accumulation should never go beyond that point. These notions are broached by their author with such sweeping negations, such wanton and insulting contempt of all existing rights, and such hostility to the prevailing convictions and institutions of mankind, both religious and civil, that even their ample promise to the depressed classes has never succeeded in conciliating to them an extensive favor.

Louis Blanc has become known to the world, not only by his theory on the organization of labor,* but by his appearance as a member of the French Provisional Government of 1848. Indeed, the persistency of his party, in attempting to carry into that national administration socialistic opinions, has been regarded as one of the efficient causes

* *Organisation du Travail.*

which divided and defeated the Republicans, restored the empire, and lifted Napoleon III. to the throne. The enemy that Louis Blanc assails, with a courage, cleverness and eloquence that have in them something admirable, is Industrial Competition. This, as it now operates, he holds to be the grand parent of all disorders, miseries and vices, and the curse of civilization. It is, he says, unfair, oppressive, foolish, selfish, sordid, jealous, mean and wicked. It is specially contrived to crush the hard-working classes. This line of vituperative assault he pursues with such spirit through a brilliant series of paradoxes and sophistries, outvying all the political economists, as to entertain the unconcerned, while his more than democratic expressions of love for the people are plainly meant to inspire them with enthusiasm. His objections overlook the law of demand and supply in labor, the stimulus competition gives to exertion, and the regular counterbalance of human desires. Thus he thinks that competition leads to the manufacture of several times as many articles as will be used, only the cheapest being bought; which does not turn out to be the fact. He thinks the workman who underbids will always get the job; whereas the quality of the work is found to have much to do with that, and men will not bid below living wages.

He thinks the bachelor will of course get the work away from the man with a wife, and still more from the man with a wife and children;—whereas it is found that a majority of men prefer a wife and children with less profit to being bachelors with more.

His favorite idea is that all men should labor from impulses of honor; that, to give them a start, the government should undertake the whole social economy, and raise a loan sufficient to support the entire working community, in public shops, till the system gets into operation. At the end of the year, the profits are to be divided into four parts, one part to go to a sinking fund to discharge the loan, another to provide a hospital for the sick and infirm, another to be kept as a reserve for special cases, and the fourth to supply the actual wants of the healthy laborers.

The only opportunity afforded the author for the proof of this plan, was in getting a large amount of tailoring done for the uniforms of the *Garde Mobile*, in the days of the republic. Fifteen hundred tailors were assembled and told that they should have two francs a day while they worked; that for all the articles made the same price should be paid as was paid to the army contractors, under the monarchy; that the total of this amount, after deducting the advance-money of fifteen hundred times two francs, should be distributed equally among the tailors. On reckoning up, at the end of the job, it was found that there were not uniforms enough made to furnish even the two francs a day. Each man seemed to think that, as all his earnings, over and above that sum, were to be so distributed that only a fifteen hundredth part of them would reach himself, there was not much motive to hurry his fingers. Louis Blanc declared, in some vexation, that the experiment was not a fair one, and was laughed at by Proudhon.

The Socialists never agree. Like Fourier, Louis Blanc ridicules and lashes St. Simon;* Proudhon ridicules and lashes Louis Blanc.† The famous double formula of Louis Blanc is this: *From every one according to his aptitudes. To every one according to his needs.* But Proudhon is acute enough to see through this, and asks, in his saucy way, "Please, Mr. Louis Blanc, who is to judge of the capacity, and of the wants? You say that my capacity is one hundred: I maintain that it is only ninety. You say that my need is ninety: I maintain that it is one hundred. Here we are differing by twenty, as to the need and the ca-

* *Histoire de Dix Ans.* Bruxelles, 1847.

† *Idée Générale de la Révolution au XIX. Siecle.* Paris, 1851

pacity. Who is to be umpire between the society and me? If the society enforces its opinion, I quit, and your association is broken. Or if I stay and succumb, your principle is broken."

Still another instructive experiment was tried by a French philosopher, a few years ago, in Algeria. Marshal Bugeaud, actuated by an ardent desire to destroy social inequalities, founded a colony for that purpose, which proved signally unsuccessful. He then wrote a candid and manly pamphlet, with this explicit testimony: "Absolute equality does not belong to this world. It is God himself that has determined this. The Socialists believe they have found equality in association; they are deceived; they will obtain only an equality of misery.*

From three sources, — Christianity, history, and the observations of common sense, — we have the means of a judgment on every community taken apart from those majestic currents of social movement, which, with their mysteriously mingled elements of the divine and human will, sweep steadily along the field of the ages. These projects are weighed in the balances; and, thus far, if not for crime, for folly, are found wanting. As a tranquil retreat for eccentric, broken-hearted, or impracticable

* *Les Socialistes et le Travail en Commun.* Paris, 1848.

people, it would seem as if there were an occasional place, in our diversified social scenery, for such establishments; only then they are not what the theorists propose. Besides, people of those classes, when huddled together without the healing and correcting influences of domestic life, are apt, as we have seen in cases near by, to turn out uncomfortable and irritating to each other, and soon to scatter in mutual disgust.*

To sum up, then, the argument: it may be objected to Communism, first, that so far as we can see, from the designs and analogies of nature, man was meant to be put in trust with personal possessions, to have them, manage them, and be answerable for them. His passions and their responsibilities, certainly, are his own, and inalienable. As Lieber has justly said, "Property is nothing else than the application of man's individuality to

* And therefore, with another, who is neither afraid of the new nor too confident of the old, "do I mistrust the theorist. He hath said in his heart that God's world, till now, hath been but a rough draft on slate, and saith that he hath a sponge. Nine times in ten doth he sit perched upon an income which is a dead branch of the living tree of industry, and spout generalities outside of the real needs of to-day. Not so, brother! This is a fight: come down and take thy side, and do battle for the most right of the two combatants. Lock up thy head, which would fain teach us that one man is more than all men; open thy heart, where there be treasures yet untold; let thy hand do with its might whatsoever it findeth to do, because idleness is the root of much evil."

external things." And a higher authority than this, while it bids us, in the Saviour's spirit of self-sacrifice, bear one another's burdens, enjoins on each of us the solemn obligation, "Every man shall bear his own burden;" and, "hast thou faith, have it to thyself."

Secondly, if property is wrong in principle, if, as Proudhon and other doctrinaires declare, "property is robbery," then the association, community, barrack or phalanx, has no right to it; and until you can get the whole human race to join the community at once, you will have one society holding property by title against the rest, and so recognizing the principle of property.

Thirdly, Communism takes away one grand stimulus to industry, the actual necessity of exertion in an honest, manly, independent struggle with the reluctances and resistances of nature, and so thwarts the ordained economy of Providence.

Fourthly, if Communism abates avarice and covetousness, as it claims, the reply is twofold: so do other and healthier forces, like Christian principle, abate and curb them; besides, it encourages other sins just as contrary to God's law and man's welfare, like sluggishness and license.

Fifthly, the ideas of Communism, by a contagion of passions, a sympathy of ideas, and a force of circumstances, too plain to require amplification of statement, tend straightway to abolish home, marriage, and purity, thus striking a blow, fatal and execrable, at the principle of personal chastity which lies at the basis of Christian civilization. Communism aims not only to regulate property and employments, but to reconstruct the domestic relations, and thus it enters the domain of morals. And if, as has been wittily but sophistically said, "the stoical scheme of supplying our wants, by lopping off our desires, is like cutting off our feet when we want shoes," the communist scheme, of regulating our desires by indulging them, is like checking a train that is running too fast down a hill by taking off the brakes.

Sixthly, the practice of the early Christians, in the primitive church, makes nothing for the Socialist's argument, since it was obviously local, temporary, adopted to meet a special exigency, and has no divine sanction.

The grand objection is, that the whole system interrupts the natural action of the laws by which God meant Society to work out the final harmony of individual and general welfare. It unsettles the balance between individual responsibility and social influence. It introduces a mechanical estimate of spiritual things. Owen betrays this materialism, perhaps inadvertently, when, in advocating the separation of children from their parents, on the ground that parental fondness stands in the way of the improvement of the offspring, he adds that parents have not the requisite machinery for the "*manufacture* of character."

Beyond question, the most comprehensive and most fatal fallacy in all Socialism is its assumption that man's highest glory is self-gratification, instead of self-control and affectionate submission to God. Here is its express denial of the central truth of Christianity. Here is its inwrought necessity of defeat.

Throwing out some unimportant schemes, like that of Pierre Leroux, the sketch I have given embraces, I believe, a notice of the principal features, though with but little of the detail, of all the more conspicuous forms that Socialist speculation has assumed. This outline, with the added reasons for distrusting them all, better exhibits both the inherent weakness in their radical principle, and the repugnance of Providence to them, than any other method of treatment I could adopt. And thus it best serves the purposes of my plan. Those divine laws, to which your attention has before been directed, as penetrating the structure of the world's Society, presiding over its progress, and determining its moral development, are adequate and immutable. By obedience to them, we render our little contribution to the sacred designs of God. All systems that fly in their face, or attempt to supersede them by mortal ingenuity, or seek to hurry too much the sublime movement of history, must perish. Room for Christian consideration of abuses, for cautious experiment, for conscientious reform, stands ever open, and the call is loud. Just where the line shall run between an effectual service of those laws and a vain innovation,—and so which of our attempts shall righteously succeed, and which shall as righteously fail, it is not for any antecedent opinion dogmatically to predict. Poised still between the good of the individual and the rights of the whole, the great welfare of the world makes its gradual advance. The religion of Christ is our absolute guide, in trying to forward it. The Almighty Father is over it, to correct our mistakes. His eternal Spirit is within it, to bear it forever on.

LECTURE VI.

SOCIETY IN RELATION TO THE INTELLECT.

It has been maintained* that Society exercises a direct formative influence, of remarkable power, on individual character,—the argument being that as human character is that product, in all his creation, on which God sets the supreme value, so the agent which is expressly adapted to develope and mould it must be one illustration of his designs. I also placed before you evidences that not only is the individual soul made receptive of this social education, but the whole social system is framed into a living network of reciprocal advantage, where, both consciously and unconsciously, but by the will of the Creator, the members of the human family mutually act and react upon one another.† In these two branches of the subject, those elements in the constitution of human nature brought especially into view, as the powers of character, were the Conscience, the Affections and the Will. It is to these interior and vital forces of man that we

* Lecture iii. † Lecture iv.

have hitherto seen Society ministering, as both their servant and their preceptor.

But there is another part of man, not yet put into particular prominence — his intellect. If it needed any affirmation of its dignity, we might find it, sufficiently, in the very terms of our general subject, which refers us not only to the Power and the Goodness, but the *Wisdom* of God. For, if we adore the wisdom in him, that is the best argument for esteeming that intellectual endowment of his creature and his child, by which the wisdom that is human is both taken in and given out. Society, in its manifold workings, and its inexhaustible demands, is a mighty helper to man's mind. It quickens and directs it. It furnishes both a stimulus and an object. The intellect is in account with Society by credit and by debt.

It would not serve either the interest or the accuracy of the treatment, to resort to the familiar psychological distributions of the faculties. What we want, rather, is to regard the mind very much as it is met and accosted by Society itself, as a vital unit,—not a mental skeleton, but an organ of life. One twofold division, however, I must ask you carefully to observe. The mind must be considered both as a recipient and as a producer; not as active and passive,—that is a common but here a false distinction. The mind is just as active in acquiring, or properly receiving, as in communicating. The old notion that the business of education is to pour facts into the pupil's memory, as oranges are dropped into a box, or merchandise is stowed in the hold of a ship, is effectually exploded. The maxim of all education that deserves the name is, Rouse the faculties, sharpen the perceptions, then spread out the orderly phenomena of nature and history, and let the hungry and discriminating intellect take hold. Knowledge is not properly acquired till it is assimilated, taken up into the soul's chyle and blood and fibre, and made a part of the juice and substance of the man. And this is no passive process. It tasks every energy; it puts all the muscles of the mind at work; it sweats its brow. Hearing a nutritious discourse, reading Plato, or Bacon, or Humboldt, learning a new language or science, should be like climbing Mount Washington, without beast or machine, on your own feet. Merely *to be instructed*, in any lawful sense of the word, is a labor.

Both as a recipient and as a producer, then, we consider the intellect to be indebted to Society. As a recipient it has Society directly and indirectly for its teacher. It is Society that organizes education,—opening the school-room or lecture-room, constructing the apparatus, providing and multiplying the materials, collecting the library. If we look at the school, the college, the institute, the lyceum, the university, the observatory, we shall see at once how impossible any such institution would be, but for that assemblage of human persons and purposes to which we have given this name,—Society. Besides, as we shall see, Society becomes, by suggestions and experiences, a more direct intellectual helper.

As a producer, the intellect finds in Society an influence that at once stimulates and guides it. The principal methods of intellectual production are conversation, specific tuition, formal discourse, authorship, and the arts of design. In each of these the mind is found in acts of expression, by signs, by language, by writing, or by color, form and sound, as in pictures, sculpture, architecture, landscape gardening, music. There is, in these, a combination of the forms of thought. There is a reconstruction of scientific facts. There is a statement of natural phenomena. There is an interpretation of laws. There is an imaginative representation of ideal truth, under the types of things that are seen and heard. These are the mind's creative operations. Often, to be sure, two processes go on together,—teaching being found one of the surest modes of learning, and the productive faculty enlarging the intuitive and receptive. Here also we have to see how, in original combinations, the intellect is urged on, provoked, directed, by the importunities and necessities of Society.

Lay the foundation of the argument, therefore, with this first principle, that God sets a positive value upon intellectual activity. I do not say, for I do not see, that we are anywhere taught that God values intellectual activity for itself alone,—as an end. He does not so value it that the mightiest mind can atone for the least moral or spiritual obliquity. He values it simply and exactly as a power. And that power, so long as the human will is free and the choice of evil is open, must be a power that works two ways, depending on a moral control. The momentum of the engine is just as effectual for mischief and disorder as for truth and right,—for Beelzebub as for Christ. Knowledge is not the world's Saviour. The kingdom of heaven is not built in the brain. Probably the saving gospel of simplicity and humility, of faith and love, hardly encounters a more unpromising or more desperate resistance than the pride, the self-sufficiency, of a congregation of intellectual sinners. And therefore I come to this topic the more gladly and eagerly, as one that lies directly on the path of one of the perilous tendencies of our times. The dogma is extant that knowledge is an ultimate good in itself, irrespective of its aims, irrespective of the question whether it has any aims, and apart from the quality of soul with which it is got and held. That doctrine terminates in one of two sorts of heathenism, — in intellectual idolatry, or else in scientific materialism. Where genius is rare, and scholars are few, there will grow up an admiring worship of colossal mental attainments. In a period of educational facilities, and the popularizing of letters, as with us, an exaggerated estimate and self-conceit of crude information will mistake knowledge for wisdom, accomplishments for virtue, till finally, the loftiest, the heroic, the spiritual objects of man are forgotten, in a sottish accumulation of private mental property, and the heart's holy loyalty is sacrificed to the arrogant aggressions of the understanding. Genius is made a gorgeous glutton, existing only for its own beatitude, and gloating over its epicurean mess. Knowledge would then be adorable for its divinity though all the heart-beats of Society were silenced, or though the beauty of the morning bloomed and brightened across a faithless world.

Nevertheless, as was said, our Creator clearly sets honor and value on the intellect in its own place,—a place high but not the highest. His designs contemplate its complete discipline and maturity. He would have every seed he has planted in humanity grow; every energy he has lodged in his children expand;—the understanding not less than the rest.

Our second position will be, that, if the Creator thus honors intellectual activity and strength, then to show that man's social nature is a regular and efficient agent for nourishing, educating, and enlarging the intellect, will be only to detect another evidence of the Almighty Presence and Design in the creation. This is what is now before us. Over against the perverted sentiment, just referred to—infidel in philosophy and idolatrous in practice—I set the conviction that the knowledge, or mental action, which does not tend to some fruitful service to men is out of harmony with Providence. Till we learn the methods, and are inspired with the passion, to reinforce and expedite our fellows, we are not truly educated, nor wise. Our minds are not working lawfully, according to their true intention. Education, in the human sense, never contemplates an isolated specimen. Its purpose is not to rear, here and there, an intellectual Peak of Teneriffe, nor to build a feudal castle of selfish learning in a desert. It groups, assimilates, fraternizes men. It achieves its end only when it has reared well-furnished, friendly laborers for the common weal.

Philosophy and fact alike justify us in pronouncing a law of reciprocal relation between the social element in man and his intellectual energy. I am aware of the liability to exaggeration of facts on the one hand, and fanciful trains of suggestion on the other, in tracing particular illustrations of this law. I do not pretend that it acts with uniform certainty or directness. I allow in advance for mixtures and exceptions. There is considerable difficulty in disentangling and tracing out the threads of an actual, secret connection, where a careless glance would see only a jumble of fortuitous coincidence. But this much, I think, can be demonstrated: Society acts on thought, as well as thought on Society. Society challenges genius, animates the understanding, fertilizes the faculty of invention, fashions the scholar. On the other hand, the disciplined and balanced mind, when it accepts its noblest commission, and moves to its divinely appointed office, becomes the helper and renovater of the race.

Before advancing a step, we must disabuse ourselves of a pedantic fallacy; the notion that all intellectual force is confined to those special forms of expression which literature has exclusively appropriated, viz., Books and the Fine Arts. These are convenient, impressive, powerful forms of mental action. But they by no means exhaust the mind's resources, nor embody all its operations. The world is stirred and carried forward by intellectual energies playing around it, which never found their way into libraries or galleries. Literature itself, properly speaking, is but a voice, not an idea, nor is it the only voice ideas utter. Ideas speak in institutions, in enterprises, in colonies, in local improvements, in governments, in commerce, in farms, in mechanism, in manners, in ceremonies and rituals of worship, in household furniture and habits, no less than in treatises and poems. Writing and the arts are but signs and exponents of that inner world of the mind, of which these other facts are signs and exponents just as much, and quite as weighty. For example, commerce is regarded, primarily, as an institution of self-interest; but the thinking merchant is a student also, and has other books than those on the shelves of his book-case. His calculations, his combinations, his sweeping surveys of countries, ports, harvests, financial causes and currents, have to move under the captaincy of the brain. What are those colossal structures, that architecture rears at his bidding along your thoroughfares, but solid treatises upon forethought and enterprise? What are those palatial vessels that glide new every week from our ship-yards, and go out to battle with elements fiercer than any veteran battalions, but thick-ribbed creations of the mind, swimming thoughts with rudders and sails, chapters of political economy written in iron and oak, speeches spoken round the globe to the oceans and continents, volumes launched and gone to sea, the circulating library of the climates? A deed is no less an intellectual birth—the product of thought—than a word. The brain goes into an heroic act as well as into an oration or a sonnet. Indeed, when the times grow earnest or revolutionary, and ideas stir most bravely, the mere *litterateur* drops out of concern. Busy hands and expanding emotions vote him an impertinence, and push him into a corner, to wait for a softer air, when the rugged emergency is over. No disparagement to Letters and Libraries; they are the text-books of the generations; they make mental treasures permanent; they hold fast what is got; they correct tradition; and sooner or later the world's best thought is reflected in that record. Only remember, intellectual activity and production begin before literature, and achieve immense conquests and benefactions outside of it.

As soon as Society begins to be, it begins to solicit and tax the human brain. Every new social want is a new spur to contrivance, to thought, to intellectual exertion. Civilization has to be built, —slowly, and expensively; and the social and intellectual forces are the contractors, in partnership. The savage must get out of his cave, under a roof, and the intellect must be a carpenter and build the roof for him. As his social condition rises, it must go on building, hut, and tent, and house, and mansion, and palace, and assembly-room, and custom house, and hall of legislation, and temple,—each in its turn and place. As primitive man lays off the apron of fig-leaves, the girdle of bark, the untanned hide of the beast, the intellect must turn tailor and adjust the fabric, and fashion the costume, of his dress. To substitute utensils for the fingers in eating, or steel hatchets for a stone in cutting, is an intellectual proceeding. So throughout. Civilization is a perpetual provocative to mental skill. Society is an unceasing beggar at the gates of Wisdom. It turns the key of knowledge. It tugs and labors at the lid of Nature's chest. It clamors for all light. It uncovers all secrets;

protests against all monopolies; and forbids Nature's children to boast, "I know something that you do not." The doctrine of intellectual reserve, as Fontenelle's maxim had it, that "if a wise man has his hand full of truths, he will open only his little finger," Society indignantly repudiates. Not only will it insist on having all that science and scholarship know published and diffused, but it goads the man of science and the scholar to know more for its sake.

To appreciate this mental stimulus from social wants, we have only to look round first upon the furnishing and the walls of our own dwellings. Here are the results of mechanical industry, guided in every manufacture by intellectual faculty. Here are fabrics that comfort the body, save and measure time, light the rooms at nightfall, set the windows that let the sunrise beckon to us in the morning, pour the pond that mirrors the mountains into our chambers, dig and forge the metals that form the implements and the coin and the plate that social necessity uses, bring the coal mine and the forest to soften the winter, spread carpets under our feet, or hang the pictured scenery of countries we never saw before our eyes.

Or else, for a more vivid and magnificent illustration yet, enter one of our annual exhibition-rooms of industry and invention,—a County Fair, or the Crystal Palace of a continent. Every such collection of workmen and their works is a social jubilee of mental victory. It is Society celebrating the Brain's Independence. The whole scene is a vital institute of intellectual instruction. It is an educator. It is an argument. It is an encyclopædia. It is a poem. It is a manual of learning. It is one of the people's quick-witted, extemporized universities. It is a school of design. It puts new illumination into old task-work; it raises the tone of life; it brightens the observer's senses. It reaches back its quickening touch into all the work-shops and factories of the land, and rouses the mind there. It helps finish and edify Society. For still the laborer is greater than the labor; the engineer is superior to the engine; the operative is of more significance than the loom; the woman is finer than her embroidery. There are the trophies of peaceful battles, which the mind, like a loyal general, having wrestled with the obstinacy of nature, brings home to its commonwealth and sovereign, Society.

There too you see how the increasing social demand brings in the inventiveness of the mind to make up for the lacking capacity of the body. Cotton cloth was once manufactured by hand, principally in the East Indies. But the widened Society of the earth grew impatient; two or three strong heads were persuaded to take the matter into their thought, and to-day a single loom-tender in Lowell can spin as much cotton in an hour as three thousand Hindoos together. There is a pyramid in Egypt which it took one hundred thousand men twenty years to build. The machinery now running in England would lift all those materials to their place in the structure, in eighteen hours. When Boulton, the engineer, went up to the palace, and came into the presence of George III., to explain to the royal dulness how that machinery might be set going, and the contemptuous king said to him, as he might to a common peddler, "Well, sir, what have you got to sell?" Boulton stood up, and said, "What kings, sire, are all fond of—power." His intellect had responded to a social want, and it made his head kinglier than the one that wore the crown.

One of the characteristics of modern industry is the division and subdivision of labor. It is an inevitable incident to the advancement of civilized Society.* At first sight, it might seem to narrow the range of the laborer's thoughts, and so to be unfavorable to the growth of the mind. Practi-

* See Plato's "Republic," Book ii., Chapter ii.

cally, however, it is found that this distribution in the departments of work is attended with increased mental aptitude and activity. It is because thoroughness and concentration are stronger intellectual attributes than versatility, or breadth of surface. The probability is that the man who should undertake to plan, frame, finish, and furnish his own house,—to be architect, mason, carpenter, blacksmith, painter, glazier, locksmith, plumber, upholsterer, in one,—would really have a less accurate and forcible mind than he who should *master* only one of those trades, and would have a much less comfortable house besides. Take up the Directory of a large city, and turn to the list of employments. See how many hands it takes to achieve the work once performed by one. Then see how much more completely, rapidly, cheaply, each part is done; how the division condenses attention, perfects execution, promotes discoveries in each line, and widens the range of competition. Then compute how many of these multiplied avocations have to do, directly or indirectly, with your own daily enjoyment; and it will become only plainer and plainer that the whole social body has a vital interest in the activity of thought.

Thus the progress of invention goes on,—intellectual energy accumulating, and reaching out on every side, stimulated by the progress of Society. But, presently, there springs up a popular alarm. The instinct of self-preservation and self-interest apprehends a danger. Will not the contrivances and mechanisms which are said to save labor, diminish also the wages of labor? Will not the machine that does the work of a hundred pairs of hands, supersede the hands, leave them idle, and the mouths they used to feed starving? A very pertinent social question: for if the apprehension is reasonable, it militates against our position, showing the intellect rather the enemy of Society than its friend.

The cases of this apparent conflict of intellectual and social laws are abundant. I can myself recall the amusing scene—indeed it was scarcely a dozen years ago—when in one of the most intelligent agricultural districts of New England, the neighbors of the venturous farmer who first bought a horse-rake refused to be convinced by the plainest proofs of its economy, but looked askance at it over the fence as an impertinent piece of agricultural heresy. They saw with their eyes that three loads of hay went into the barn in the same time that it took to gather one with the old rakes, yet prejudice was stronger than sight, and the pupil of the eye was a pupil that would not go to school. The old spirit is by no means dead, which has persecuted the prophets, and ridiculed the thinkers, and starved the innovaters; which, in the old world, has often collected a rabble to mob a new discovery that came to Society with healing on its wings; which forbade Watt to open his instrument shop in Glasgow; which sneered at "Fulton's folly," as the first steamboat was nicknamed in Brown's shipyard, at New York; which actually broke the heart of poor William Lee, in the time of James I., driving him by English indifference to France, and then by French bigotry from Rouen to Paris, where he died in misery, because the world would not let its stockings be made by his stocking-machine; which, in South America, according to Humboldt, instigated the citizens to petition the government against the building of a road among the Andes, lest it should damage the interests of the carriers who had enjoyed the monopoly of carrying travellers across the mountains in baskets strapped on their backs; which inflamed the Swiss peasants, when they saw Rupp constructing the superb slide of Alpnach for bringing down the pine timber of Mount Pilatus into Lake Lucerne, to accuse his trigonometry of being the instigation of Satan; which, only forty years ago, threw brickbats at a collier in Philadelphia who brought down nine wagon loads of mountain coal to sell, hooting after him as an impostor that pretended to sell stones for fuel; which trembled, all the way from Boston to Albany, when the Western railroad was about to be laid, with the ludicrous fear that horses would go out of fashion, and have to be shot down in their shoes as a drug; which drove Hargreaves and his spinning-machine out of Lancashire for his life, and prompted Laurence Earnshaw to break up his own machine in a fit of benevolent apprehension lest he should take bread out of his neighbors' mouths, although a bold improvement on both their designs by Arkwright afterwards gave wages and food to millions of workmen, raised the commerce in cotton from *two* million pounds a year to a thousand millions of pounds, and poured wealth into the treasury of the nation and the world.

That timid temper is not exterminated yet. And therefore it is right to assert that the social welfare, and God's plans for it, really justify all manner of intellectual originality; to demonstrate the absolute social justice of the industrial and intellectual laws. It is capable of demonstration, that the multiplying of labor-saving machinery never diminishes the means of living; in fact, that labor is not finally saved, but multiplies itself, by and in the machine. The final cause of labor-saving contrivances is to increase labor. This is the eternal paradox of the world's growing civilization. The several industries of mankind move forward under one harmonious plan. Every legitimate development or production in one favors the others. I know of nothing in the whole history of men more beautiful or more majestic than the certainty of this rule. The illustrations of it are the annals of all the arts. Apart from its own fascinating interest, it is one of the most splendid proofs of the Being and Providence of God. The family of men are under one Father. It is as sure as gravitation, that every fresh mechanism he puts into the world through an ingenious intellect, he takes up and makes a part of his unimpeachable Goodness toward our race. Its inconveniences are local and temporary; its beneficence is cosmopolitan and permanent. It enriches, employs, establishes, equalizes. It creates demands only to satisfy them; it saves expenditure only to scatter it with a wider sweep. A few copyists are at first set adrift by the printing-press; but what an army of operatives that mighty engine nourishes to-day!—a stupendous philanthropist of employment, if that were its only function. The sewing-machine may bring a brief embarrassment to the poor seamstress; let thoughtful Charity consider it, and soften the transition; but in the end she also will be the stronger and better for it if she only keeps her own mind up with the times. If she sits sullenly down and complains, or persists in making her fingers competitors of wheels and spindles, she will be crushed. There is less stitching to be done, that her faculties may be liberated for larger enterprises, and her hands find a more exalted ministry. It is futile to be jealous of the necessities of progress. We must all go where the Almighty points, and not ask to have the orbs of celestial light stand still for our private accommodation. We must be hospitable and brave in our welcome of the new Future, as well as thankful venerators of the old Past.

By such a course of reflection as this, that very fact which we have seen cited as an objection to our doctrine becomes, instead, an argument for it. That feeling, that prejudice, which opposes the generous and progressive application of science to the arts and conveniences of human life is found to be, not the friend but the foe of Society, not a social but a selfish instinct. Private monopoly, class interests, sectional privilege, may well be jealous of intellectual light and power; but when we rise to consider the whole family of man, and look abroad on the wide wants of the world, we find the exact terms of our proposition reëchoed everywhere. Society is the providential nutriment, motive, theatre and rewarder of the intellect, hardly less than of the heart.

Furthermore, it is because man in his social nature is actuated so largely by his heart, and because it is a principle of our nature that the heart warms and quickens the head, that this action of Society on the intellect takes place. It was a maxim of the great historian of the church, Neander, that even of a theologian the heart is the determining agent: *Pectus theologum fecit.* Doubtless it would have been better for the church if this natural and beautiful intention had not met so many obstacles from dogmatism and ambition. But I believe there is no considerable field of human life where we cannot gather testimony that both the acquisitive and the creative faculties are set free and quickened through the affections. And, for obvious reasons, the most familiar instances will be the most effectual for our purpose.

Take common conversation. We do not duly consider the amount of real intellectual activity and originality that are constantly brought into play through talk, dialogue, rejoinder, repartee,—

in households, on the street, in the encounters of company. Probably more good things are said every day, and vanish into air, than can be found printed in any library in the world. Now observe that this animation and brilliancy of conversation are apt to be very much in proportion as the social intercourse is free, untrammeled, simple and cordial; very much as the feelings and affections have an unobstructed and unembarrassed play; very much, in other words, as Society is most social. Conventionalism, fashion, ceremony, the stiff drawing-room parades where people march out like walking lay-figures, or clothes-horses only as frames to exhibit dress, or to perform grimace and mutual make-believe hospitality, — these yield no bright talk. They benumb the intellectual faculty, or drive it out of the house. Even eloquent persons grow tedious, and the nimblest parts are dumb. "Good society have I seen," said Goethe, —"good society they call it, though there is not in it the material for the smallest of poems." But on the other hand, where the company have the most mutual confidence, the most mutual affinity, the most love,—which are the specific elements of the social nature, — there thought will strike out its images of boldest character, and conversation will weave its finest charm.

Why is it, in respect of personal social success, that with one man, or one woman, all your powers of expression are locked up, as in frost, the moment you approach? There is no such thing as communication; every topic is barren; every sentence comes "wrong end first;" the air between you seems to be a non-conductor; the interview is desperately dull; while with another, all is lucid, suggestive, and fruitful; the very same topics are radiant; your phrases come from you with unwonted point and finish, and your own fluency surprises you. Why is this, except that the emotional and sympathetic part of our nature, that on which social life depends, is rich in one case, and in the other poor? Where there is nothing *in common* between people, there can be nothing *communicated*. Where there is no oil of friendly joy to anoint the metallic and rusty hinges of the mind, every movement will creak, and stick, and jar.

Popular oratory exhibits the same thing. It is the assembly that animates the speaker, and whether he writes for them, or thinks into speech before them, stimulates his invention. Very often it is the audience that makes the oration: the brilliant and responsive throng that kindles the fire of the speech. The parliament, the forum, the hustings, are not only educators, but electric batteries. Even that resonant, reverberating eloquence of Demosthenes himself, which

> "Wielded at will that fierce democracy,
> Shook th' arsenal, and fulmined over Greece,
> To Macedon, and Artaxerxes' throne,"

would not have sounded down the centuries, but for the social passions of the tribunal and agora of Athens. So of the whole inspired line of orators that he heads. Eloquence is a social product.

Undoubtedly we must try these principles by that which has come to be known in the world as literary history. We must ask if the intellectual princes and giants have owed anything to Society. Many people do not admit anybody to belong to the kingdom of the intellect, except technical authors and artists. The argument will bear the strain put upon it even by that theory. Doubtless there are exceptional instances, of men whose natures were so solitary, or their brain so dominant and overbearing, that their greatness would appear with little social excitement. Yet, even these, if you trace causes closely enough, will be found indebted to the currents of human sympathy. Mr. De Quincey divides intellects into two classes, —laborers of the mine and laborers of the mint.

The one class dig truth up, or discover it; the other strike, cast, mould it into coin for current use. Both are amenable to the state of Society they live in, and are partly the creatures of its past action. The powers of the greatest men are heightened by their acting on people about them. They see their gifts reflected in the popular enthusiasm. They hear the acclaim of the popular voice. They feel the responsive thrill of the public pulse. This reduplication of individual energy by social sympathy is one of the first laws of intellectual life. Every mind gains force by seeing the fruits of its force. Science, for the quickness, decision, and systematic arrangement of its teachers, stands under patent obligations to the mutual attitude of pupil and professor, reader and author, hearer and speaker. In the strong metaphor of that competent authority, Niebuhr, they that are taught become to him that teaches his wings,—and not only his wings but his feet, and his hands, and his eyes. I am happy to cite to the same conclusion the opinion of a writer who has reflected so carefully and comprehensively on the subject of civilization as M. Guizot. "If a man makes a mental advance," says he, "if he acquires some new idea, or some new faculty, what is the desire that takes possession of him at the very moment he makes it? It is the desire to promulgate his sentiment to the exterior world—to publish and realize his thought. He feels obliged, impelled, as it were, by a secret interest, to extend, to carry out of himself, the melioration which has been accomplished within him. To what but this do we owe the exertions of great reformers,—those benefactors of the human race who have changed the face of the world?"

Then, in point of fact, we see prodigious effects wrought on both the views and the abilities of eminent thinkers by the state of Society in which they lived, or out of which they grew. Every chapter of literary history, from Plutarch to the American Encyclopædia, from Hesiod to Wordsworth, supports this statement. Signal epochs in letters have commonly been inaugurated by some invigorating revolution in the elements of human life. Sometimes these movements have been made the subjects of great literary works. Sometimes they have only acted on susceptible organizations, as by electrical excitement. The re-asserted instincts of liberty and equality re-appear in sublimer statues and pictures and buildings, in wider and deeper philosophies, in eloquence that commands broader auditories, in poetry that burns with more of the immortal fire. The revolutionary and the constitutional period each has its appropriate and typical intellectual tone. If Patrick Henry, then Webster. A grand history raises grand historians. Given Achilles and Hector, and sooner or later a Homer must be. Herodotus comes of Xerxes. The genuine hero will get his story told, his acted music sung. On the pages of Thucydides the pathos and tragedy of civil war utter their august grief, and the speeches of warrior-statesmen find a fit setting in the stately narrative. The vast tides of the world's life, as if by a wonderful instinct of self-preservation, cast up their own painters and chroniclers. Every large interest or passion finds a voice. A conservative aristocracy does not lack a fastidious Pindar, and a courtly Sir Walter Scott, nor a discontented democracy its Victor Hugo and Rienzi. The decline of Athenian manners and the degeneration of woman commission a comedian like Aristophanes. When an artificial civilization in Greece or Great Britain makes it possible for a sharp, cold, brilliant banterer to be the great man, Menander or Thackeray is there. Stern and calculating Rome will have no comedy at all; for it has neither laughter nor leisure; the grim fights of gladiators are its unsmiling sport, and its nearest approach to mirth is the sardonic savageness of satire. But, nevertheless, the greatness of all Roman writing is the ever present idea of Rome, a Society of men. The Augustan age there, and the Elizabethan in England, were times of the growth of social empires. Men's minds heaved unconsciously with the pulsations of youthful commonwealths. Periods of ardent patriotism are almost always intellectual harvests. A social energy is at work which liberalizes and expands. It opens the self-occupied understanding with ideas of a political Brotherhood, and common sufferings and hopes. In one country, and that not the one feeling the primary shock, we see the French Revolution rousing such a senatorial order as Herder and Goethe, Klopstock, Kant, Schiller and Humboldt.

We speak much of the benefits brought to the human intellect by the invention of Printing. It flashed in a wave of light on the race, which spreads forever, and brightens as it spreads. A careful study of European history, however, during the period immediately preceding that great epoch, shows that even that vast engine would have been powerless but for the mighty preparations of change that had been slowly working in the bosom of European society. The struggle between individual ambition and the overgrown estates of the feudal aristocracy had not been in vain. The lower classes began to be lifted. The sense of personal liberty had awaked. Mercantile wealth was increased. Independence came with it. Trading towns became the seats of liberal ideas, and raised a barrier of free competition against hereditary privilege. And so, when Printing came, it found a new order of Society ready to receive it. Doubtless this new order had more to do than was apparent with the invention itself. At any rate, it was the arm of strength that sent its benefits abroad, and gave its impulse to the continent.

Could we only look far enough down into the underlying causes of things, and read the world's story with these in view, we should see how human wants are thus the begetters of intellectual power. Before a great man appears, there are hidden causes, working in the bosom of God's social family, that require him. He never comes till he is wanted, though the world, stoning its prophets still, often misinterprets its hunger, and knows not what it wants. Every splendid discovery is wrung out of reluctant, inexhaustible nature at the cry of a mortal desire. Not more certainly is the planet built for man, than every new intellectual birth in it is a straight answer to his solicitation. The religion of Judea and the Norse manhood,—Love and Strength, or Heart and Will,—

met and married on the old Roman hearth-stone, to generate a new line of ideas no less than of persons. Copernicus came to find the physical centre, just when the dawning truths of science began to require that the axle-point of the heliocentric system should be fixed. The age of Raphael opened just when the rough lineaments of western civilization supplicated, inarticulately, the refining graces of Christian art. Columbus was but the finger of one crowded continent feeling after room and rights in another,—after an industrial America to atone for military Europe, a missing hemisphere to finish the globe. Lord Bacon was the answer of tired scholasticism begging to get out of the labryrinth into a simple path. A hurrying century felt hindered in its restless emigration and enterprise, and Fulton came up to help it along. Busy and related, yet widely divided communities, ached for instant communication, and Franklin found, and Morse equipped the nimble medium that should set them talking face to face. Luther was a pioneer pushed on by the impatient hopes of stifled millions, — a wrestler with the hierarchy, borne forward by the consecrating prayers of an army of "reformers before the Reformation."

Then, in all those emanations of thought where the emotions play, the efficiency of humane causes is only the more palpable and characteristic. Masters of poetry, romance, arts of design, have been the spokesmen of social experience. In their moments of free insight, liberated from the dullness of gross outsides, and from the caprices of fashion, they have gone down into the abiding deeps within, and spoken out of them. That is to be a genius. In that sense, all the eternal voices are *de profundis.* Orators are only the pleaders of passions and convictions, with passions and convictions just like themselves. Musical composers sing the sorrow and joy of the children of men. Tragedy is but the wail of some spiritual pain. The soul's long warfare with conventional restraints, with foes of circumstance, with the tyranny of custom, with the baffling of love or aspiration,—with some slow Iliad of calamities, or grim Inferno of conscience, — this is the ever-living and ever-commanding theme of all inspiring speech.

Indeed, we may treat the whole world of letters as a drama in itself. The unity, the postures, the dialogue, the progress from a Chaldean exordium to a divine conclusion, all are there, or will be. What we call history is but the marginal annotation,—the explanatory argument. Treatises, orations, sermons, volumes, are the talk of the lengthened colloquy. The drama is the most perfect form of writing, precisely because it is closest to the actual and social life of men. In Æschylus and Shakspeare the agents of power are not the transient interests or qualities of class, rank or age, but the royal emotions and passions of essential humanity. In the characters, situations, sufferings, it is not princes, nor generals, nor demigods, that arrest our breath, but men and women like ourselves. If kings, lords, queens, dukes, cardinals come before us, it is still as men and women that they come, and concern us. Regality, titles, sceptres, are only the means of operating the human nature which they accidentally attend. The emperor himself is but the "usher that doth go before" that more imperial presence, the soul. Hence these *confidantes* of nature tell us more than we knew about our own economy,—tell us "the secrets of our own bosoms."

Turn now to the other side of this mutual inter-action between Learning and Life, or Ideas and Society. The proposition is that thinking and studying men do not fulfil their final and predestined office, till they reach the vital springs of action, and create an ampler and freer style of being,—till they ennoble Society, elevate its estate, purify its relationships, and dignify its manners. Kings, like Alfred sitting out his eight nightly hours, after harassing days, for classical study, to rouse some ambition in his stupid people, when not a priest south of the Thames could translate the Latin prayers he repeated in public,—priests like Archbishop Bruno of Cologne, studying new languages for the enlightening of his flocks,—these are patterns of the disinterested scholar,—true kings and priests, not reigning in the etiquette of courts or the ceremonial of a hierarchy, but in the grand commonwealth of man, in the living church of God. The educated, scholarly, brotherly man is the ordained hierophant and crowned law-giver of the race.

The course of literary progress from the first has been towards a heartier recognition of the worth and needs of the common people. In this, the advance of thought has followed the Christian gospel,—preached first to the people. This tendency must have free, open way. Then, as has been somewhere said, in the beautiful unfolding and circuit of the perfect plan, Literature, which began by bringing mistaken deities to earth, completing its celestial mission, returns and lifts an instructed Society to heaven. Wisdom is always bending to ignorance, not in patronage but in respect, and beckoning it upward. As the poet prays, "Bodies bright, and greater, serve the less not bright," which is but a paraphrase of the apostolic charity; "Ye that are strong ought to bear the infirmities of the weak." We read the destiny of our multiplied appliances of culture in the best instincts of the acquiring mind. And whether, with the elder generations, we interpret that destiny in the light of a golden age, lying, like an island of the blest, before us, or, with Plato, "resolve the soul's purest thoughts into remembrances of a brighter life, already passed in a nobler society," we find the predicted issue to be the same,—a kingdom of heaven on the earth.

Knowledge, to become wisdom, needs to let the heart beat in its breast,—to be what humanity asks of it,—not a sallow monk dreaming in a clammy cave, not a selfish sybarite gloating over its dish of delicious reputation, not a paramour dallying with the passions, not a respectable servant-in-waiting keeping the door of pompous patrons, not a mystic dervish gazing complacently on itself, but the breathing, sympathizing, and whole-souled benefactor of the people.

There is a glorious possibility, which has sometimes haunted the dreams of thinkers, at whose grandeur all common hopes of scholars kneel with veneration. It is the unity of all sciences, arts, labors, letters, under one all-embracing and connecting principle, or law. If that majestic idea shall ever be realized, what shall be the one unifying truth? What girdle shall be elastic enough to encircle all knowledge? What principle shall be vast enough to contain all systems, schools, discoveries, conclusions, clasping with its starry belt all the constellations of human thought? I answer, it is no other, it can be no other, than the Brotherhood of social men, beneath the Fatherhood of God.

Here, then, is our conclusion: the world's thinkers and students are its natural menders and movers, because they are the quickeners and guides of its actors. New greatness awaits the human mind, as it shall more and more practically confess this truth and become the willing servant of the wants and welfare of Society. Take Philosophy. Is it not in the nature of things that her soul should expand,—for she, too, has a soul,—when she turns her discoveries into treasures of mercy, and then scatters them by the waysides of common men, and at the doors of the poor, dispelling superstition, cheapening comforts, easing drudgery, making herself the "Guide of Life?" The Arts: can they help springing into more vigorous and graceful activity, when they feel themselves to be like ministering spirits, public pleaders for faith and love,—beckoning, with their elevating forms of beauty, to the children of ignorance and crime, and calling them up to visions of refinement, purity and truth? Poetry must ever gain most complete control of men's hearts when it sings the tragic *Miserere* over bruised and baffled affections, or strikes the note of *Exultemus* and *Gloria in excelsis* at the righteous emancipation of the oppressed. Even the mastery of old languages becomes a more living and engaging thing, when we hearken to these tongues of departed tribes, as to solemn, musical monitors how the everlasting policy and true honor of nations are not war but peace, not aggression but service, not oppression but freedom. Then they are not dead languages but alive again. Under a scholarship broad and bountiful as this, publishing glad tidings like the beautiful feet of Morning upon the mountains, the real golden age, at once classic and Christian, should be inaugurated by a Pentecost of Thought, Labor, and Love.

Before these kindling prospects of enlightening and redeeming Society, — which ever appeals and entreats for this intellectual ministry, — how do all other motives to mental toil sink down! The finest gold is dim. Ambition's most resplendent crown is cheap, and the sound of Fame's silver trumpet dies away. Educated men are invited to unprecedented honor, the honor of creating a Society where education shall be universal. Renouncing selfish emulation, forgetting the rivalries of schools and the bigotries of sects, they enter into a fraternity of hope and faith, "Brethren of the Misericordia" to all the ignorance and shame that still fringe our civilization, apostles of a new order, builders of a society for the Son of God. With such consecrations of the human mind, there is no destiny, dreamed or prophesied, too auspicious for the race. Learning would become the preceptor of industry, the crown of enterprise, the dignity of commerce, the ornament of the republic. Art, handmaid of refinement, — Science, interpreter of nature, — Literature, the voice of experience, — and Philosophy, the guide of life, would combine their constructive offices for rearing the open university, home, temple of the children of men. And in building that tabernacle, Thought and Love, —Intellect and Faith, our prophet and our priest,— should do all things for Society after the pattern shown them in the mount,—the mount of the vision, and adoration, of the Wisdom, and the Power, and the Goodness of God.

LECTURE VII.

SOCIETY SUBJECT TO A LAW OF ADVANCEMENT.

Everything indicates that the Creator has placed his human family on the globe for their education into a destiny which no member of that family is able to conceive. "Man," says Michelet, "is a pilgrim by nature; it is long since he set out, and I know not when he will arrive." Of this education, all the voices, the instruments, and the forces, must be found in three regions; within man himself, in the creation around him, or in the spiritual world above him. These three exhaust every possible resource for him: Humanity, Nature, Heaven.

The first of these, including the powers that reside within man himself, we must divide into two parts,—of those which pertain to man as an individual, and those that belong to him as social, or by virtue of the connection of one life with another. Where all these educating agents should have coöperated, in unbroken harmony, there man would be, in the accommodated and human sense of the term, perfect. For an expression of that possibility, sufficiently guarded and yet sufficiently positive, we may borrow the language of Robert Southey: "I am fully convinced that a gradual improvement is going on in the world, has been going on from its commencement, and will continue till the human race shall attain all the perfection of which it is capable in this mortal state. This belief is a corollary deduced from the whole history of mankind."

And since that complete condition, or indeed any tolerable approach to it, would unquestionably be a society, we are right in seeking what those social capabilities and operations are, which point to such a state, and tend towards it. We shall find that all the other forces which help and advance man,—in God, in nature, or in himself,—presuppose him to be a social creature, and act upon him as such. We shall find, further, that wherever his social conditions and faculties are most generously unfolded, there he rises steadily towards the best accomplishment of his being. These two propositions signify what I mean by the statement that Society holds in it the laws of its own progression. In the last Lecture, we saw Socialism, in all its forms, trying to hasten this movement by artificial arrangements, but blundering and failing. Nevertheless, the movement proceeds.

Two facts, respecting the much abused subject of human progress, must be frankly conceded at once. The progress is not as yet universal, as to the world's surface, nor uniform, as to its own rate of speed.

It is not universal, as to space. Probably there is as thorough degradation, attended with all the crimes, sottishness and stupidity of the savage state, on our globe to-day, as at any moment since Adam. In some dreary districts, it is plain enough, the course is steadily downward, and a higher civilization sinks to a lower. Glance at some of the great features and epochs of domestic existence. There are places, to-day—as among the Rajpoots in India—where infant children, just tasting of the life God gave to be a blessing and a joy, are miserably slaughtered to dismiss them from a more miserable lot. Sometimes, by the most horrible of maternal profanities, the poor mother spreads poison on her breast, and the babe drinks death "where nature had planted the streams of life." There are places, to-day—as among the Pawnees—where womanhood is reckoned a disgrace, and where she who receives, by her nature, most of the divine spirit into her heart, is the abject, beaten, and incredibly burdened slave of her pagan tyrant, man. In Australia, to-day, when a lover selects the maiden he would marry, this is the method of his courtship. He watches till he finds her in some solitary place, rushes at her unexpectedly, strikes her to the ground with a club or wooden sword, beats her over the head till she is senseless, drags her to his quarters, and, with these impressive proofs of affection, proposes; and, what is equally remarkable, is commonly accepted! The course of wedded love is said to be much in keeping with the gallantry of these advances. The Papuans of New Guinea sell their own children into slavery. The demonstrations of hospitality and of emotion are ludicrously inverted. When some of the New Zealanders meet their relations,—after a separation,—they face each other, join their noses, and in that position sob and howl half an hour. If there is a large group of connections to one new-comer, all but the nearest relative lay hold of the hands, shoulders and feet, leaving to the "chief mourner" in the solemnities the delicate monopoly of the nose, the rest keeping time, in a chorus of whimper, groan and yell, with him. There are places, too, where, when the last act comes, which is solemn everywhere, the naked, crouching corpse is bound with thongs of bark, crushed into a hole in the ground, thinly covered, and forsaken. I need not multiply examples of the savagery that lingers yet in the world. Does it invalidate our position, that Society is naturally progressive? If it could be known that in those regions, what we have proclaimed as the social principles, were kept, it would unquestionably invalidate it. But since it is in those places that these principles have been persistently and grossly broken, the degradation, and even the deterioration, only illustrates our doctrine, and confirms it. Man has become unnatural.

It ought to be further remarked here that our doctrine by no means involves the supposition that the course of mankind has been progressive from the beginning. On the contrary, though the point is ably disputed, the facts seem rather to instruct us that the race has suffered a vast degeneracy from a primeval social state of comparative purity. The most comprehensive students of this subject, those that include the teachings of Scripture among their *data*, agree in the opinion forcibly stated by Chalmers and others, that civilization never arose spontaneously from a state of barbarism, but was always imported, or created by contact with a people in whom the influence of an enlightened religion, or early revelation, had not been lost. "Savage man is a degenerated animal." God did not form man a savage. "There was an aboriginal civilization, coeval with the true knowledge of the true God."

The other fact I allude to is that the progress of the different branches of civilization is not uniform, though it *is progress* on the whole. Their growth is not simultaneous; nor do they expand by any law of definite proportions, like the branches of a tree, where, if one twig is lengthened a foot, a smaller twig is sure to be lengthened by a fixed fraction of a foot. Energy and taste, invention and veneration, machinery and poetry, do not advance with equal step, nor, in any particular period, is it possible to detect any established ratio between their several rates. For example, in the era of the Roman empire, the will was developed; everything else bent to the iron discipline of a military force. It was the age of armies. The Greek mind labored after the perfect in form. That was an age of ideality. For a long time after the recognition of Christianity by the civil power, from the fourth century forward, the active mind of Europe was compacting a splendid system of church unity, binding a network of ecclesiastical dependencies, under a comprehensive Christian hierarchy. For several centuries preceding and including the thirteenth, the chief business of the foremost nations seems to have been to bring out and cultivate, often in rude shapes, a certain order of high sentiments, such as loyalty, honor, class fidelity, and the enthusiasm of charity. This was the age, therefore, of the crusades, chivalry and religious houses. The sixteenth and seventeenth centuries were memorable for the resistance of the human mind to overgrown authority, and the emancipation of the individual from arbitrary despotisms in the state and the church. This, accordingly, was the age of Protestantism, Puritanism, and the settlement of New England. Afterwards, in the eighteenth century, Thought was busy pushing its new ideas out into various practical consequences, as well as into extreme speculations. And so it became an age at once of political revolutions and of philosophical scepticism. Perhaps it would be an unwarrantable presumption to venture on a general designation of what the special office of our own age is. To take a broad view of its characteristics, we need to stand less than is now quite possible under the confusing influence of those passing interests which may be transient in the eyes of Omniscience, or even of posterity, while they look colossal in their relation to our limited faculties. The errand of our time *appears* to be, to push out into more extensive applications the tendencies of the two centuries immediately preceding,—especially into the two directions of political reform, and the practical machinery of life, under a diffused education. Probably in a future not very distant, and possibly through unprecedented conflicts, a more settled order of society, on a new basis, with institutions incorporating the new ideas, the secrets extorted by all these struggles, may appear,—the ancient stability enclosing the results of the modern agitation,—the kingdom that was to come. These several ages that I have thus referred to are not distinctly marked off, with an exact beginning and end, in their events and spirit and character, as they are in tables of chronology.* One period is shaded into another, and the work of each laps over upon those adjacent.

In the divine plan, each epoch has its task,—sometimes an original one, sometimes merely to further, or to correct, one that has gone before. We learn that the progress of the species is not the simple motion of a single body, passing straight forward, faster or slower, like a ball over a plane

* "There is no epoch in which one idea rules alone, to such an extent that no other idea might seem to exist."

See Cousin, in his "History of Modern Philosophy," Lecture VII., second series, where he refers to his great Division of History into the three epochs—the epoch of the Finite, of the Infinite, and of the Relation of the Two.

surface, or a car on rails; but it is a motion compound, broken, scattered. We must compare it, not to an organized army drawn up in ranks, with the drilled precision of officered regiments and brigades, with vanguard, main body, rear guard and wings, and marching on towards a definite station; but rather to a loose company of adventuring emigrants, exploring an unknown country, feeling their way into a wilderness, — made up of different bodies,—with light scouts to reconnoitre, but often obliged to turn back,—with slow escort and heavy teams to bring on the baggage, some repelled by the obstinacy of nature from positions they have occupied to take more circuitous routes, others waiting at advanced posts for the remainder to come up, but all animated by one common purpose urging them, at whatever hazards and through whatever difficulties, as the law of their life, to press on. Says the author of "Friends in Council," "The progress of mankind is like the incoming of the tide, which, for any given moment, is almost as much of a retreat as of an advance; but still the tide moves on."

Of this Progress there are certain prominent instruments, or agents, contained in the very structure of Society, and parts of its vital system. Some of these have been sufficiently exhibited already. At this point, however, others come into view, and must be mentioned.

One of these is the perpetual system of variety of personal abilities that nature keeps up in the social world. Always there are some stronger to help the infirmities of the weak; always there are weak to be quickened and forwarded by the strong. There are wise and ignorant; there are needy and abounding; there are ugly and beautiful; there are impulsive and calculating, phlegmatic and mercurial, practical and imaginative, logical and intuitive, taciturn and talkative. Always, by the benign and beautiful balancings of the Father's will, the old and the young, full strength and little children, grey locks and the soft hair of infancy, are on the earth together. The more we explore what is continually wrought and evoked, of human power and goodness and wisdom, by these diversified and unequal relations, the more we shall see that they form one of the prolific generators of an advancing spirit in the race.

Secondly, there is the characteristic of hereditary transmission. What one generation gains it can hand over, in large part, to its successors, in knowledge, aptitude, skill. How broadly distinguished, in this regard, is man from any of the inferior animals! We saw that there is no society among them. They transmit nothing. With each individual specimen, all that he did perishes. Even if some slight material structure of his building-instinct survives, the *nidus* of the offspring has to be fabricated anew. "There are no birds in last year's nest." The instincts are resupplied to every individual of his kind,—no more, no less. But humanity holds by a longer title. Much as man takes with him to the grave, he leaves much behind. In the matured records and accumulations of his skill, in the raised and quickened capacity of his nature, in physiological, intellectual, moral traits, there is a solemn, a fearful, a precious hereditary law. And the more it comes to be recognized and revered, the more rapidly will mankind move and mature.

"Be assured," says Ruskin, "that all the best treasures of this world are not to be produced by each generation for itself; but we are all intended, not to cover our work in snow that will melt, but each and all of us to be rolling a great gathering snow-ball, higher and higher along the Alps of human power. Thus the science of nations is to be accumulative, from father to son; each learning a little more and a little more; each receiving all that was known and adding its own gain. The history and poetry of nations are to be accumulative, — each generation treasuring the history and the songs of its ancestors, and adding its own history and its own songs. And the art of nations is to be accumulative, just as science and history are,—the work of living men not superseding but building itself upon the work of the Past. For the intention of Providence concerning that art is evidently that it should all grow together in one mighty temple, — the rough stones and the smooth all finding their place, and rising, day by day, in richer and higher pinnacles to heaven."

Another of the inwrought signs and means of progression in the social nature is the obvious tendency of communities to store up and preserve what they have gained, in institutions; institutions of learning, of traffic, of defence, of manufacture, of government, of charity, of worship. They make institutions for the intellect, institutions for the passions, institutions for the interests, institutions for the brain, the heart and the hand. They are always funding their stock. Society has a manifest genius for organization. When it gets a good thing it puts it into a shape where it will keep, and be reproduced. These institutions, whether educational, industrial, moral or religious, have a wonderful working and creative energy. They reduplicate human strength. Hence it is that most

men like to work in and with institutions. They feel that they borrow, and expend, and are backed up by, a great invested ability beyond their own; and that their own is vastly multiplied by the machine it goes into. Hence the man whose foresight or benevolence founds a durable institution becomes the greatest of benefactors. It goes on, in some measure, of itself. Next after personal character it is the most efficient of all agencies on earth; and very often it acts over a wider surface than personal character can, and makes that also more fruitful. I place, therefore, among the inherent proofs of its natural progressiveness, this disposition of Society to embody and perpetuate its acquisitions in instituted forms.

Put with this, however, a law equally clear, and potent, and progressive. Society not only puts on institutions when it wants them; it puts them off when it has done with them,—when they are only crusts, dried shells, enclosing no life, or manacles and fetters, cramping and distorting the life they cannot contain. In some of its temporary stages, the functions of Society, says Herbert Spencer, are fulfilled "by appliances destined to disappear as fast as the ultimate appliances become efficient. Associated humanity has larval appendages, analogous to those of individual creatures. As in the common Triton of the ponds the external lungs dwindle away when the internal lungs have grown to maturity; and as, during the embryo state of the higher *vertebrata*, temporary organs appear, serve their purpose awhile, and then are reabsorbed, leaving only signs of their having been, — so, in the earlier forms of the body politic, do there exist institutions, which, after answering their ends for a time, are superseded and become extinct." The new spirit pushes off the old form.

Another proof is the propensity to traffic, — a constant stimulus to invention, to skill, to enterprise, to adventure. Doubtless the commerce in merchandise is inferior to the commerce in ideas; yet we ought to remember how often the one has been the carrier and mail-bag of the other; how the ships of the merchant have exported and imported knowledge and refinement. The individual traders thought little of this; they were looking after their own fortunes, and driving their own bargains;—all the more it shows God's law above them, making them its unconscious agents. Obeying that eager commercial passion, in oriental antiquity, the nations broke over their narrow boundaries, learned each other's secrets, imbibed a more catholic spirit. In the middle ages, the caravans of transportation bore intellectual vitality from city to city, and stirred the stagnant populations. In modern times, the seats of commerce have been proverbially the seats of liberty, and the sails of fleets have been the wings of liberal thought.

Still another of these agents is travel. By virtue of his social constitution man is a travelling animal, — and, in turn, the more he travels the more Society is advanced. It is plain enough why nature set man on his legs, and lent to head and heart, stomach and spine, a locomotive energy. And yet it has come about, in the tremendous outward aggressive pressure of his itinerant habits, that his legs are now the least part of his locomotive apparatus. He makes all the elements of earth and air and water move, pull, push, swing, float, gallop, propel him. People make roads, ferries, ships; and then roads, ferries, ships, make the people. Every time a rustic countryman goes to the next large town, every time an American goes to Europe, unless there is an unwonted perverseness in his stupidity, he comes back with a wider mind. No wonder the Greeks put their highways under the protection of their deities, — for though their gods did not succeed much better as superintendents of streets than as patterns of righteousness, it indicated the popular estimation. When barbarism first overran Italy, true to the destructive instinct, the woodsmen demolished the highways; but they had to build them again. What if the great Egyptian and Roman roads were first made for the march of armies? After the armies, apostles. Mark the steps. First the pack-horse and the mule; then the two-wheeled sledge, dray, waggon, which, clumsy as it was, was estimated to multiply power on the whole, in a tenfold ratio. The first iron road for steam carriages was not opened in England till thirty years ago, and in France but five years earlier. You see already what a civilizer it is. Motion is freedom, and science, and wealth, and brotherly love. The engine and rail are more effectual anti-slavery lectures than the most eloquent of the Anti-Slavery Society's agents. They call out great men, and make small men greater. Up in the woods of northern New York is a young boy whose brain is full of possible mathematics. It would all perish in him, but the railroad lays hold of him, draws him to Yale or Harvard, and he carries forward the computations of Bowditch and La Place. Not by direct intention, but secretly in the plans of Providence, every spade that the laborer, at the bidding of social need, strikes into the bank to level it for the engineer, every trowel that masonry plies on the culvert and bridge, every hammer that welds the machinery of the locomotive, every bolt that rivets the ship-timber, bears its part in the carving and the architecture of a better Future. Over these iron paths God will roll in upon us an age of greater toleration, helpfulness, love; and, by the simplest mechanism that art is perfecting, new disciples and prophets, faithful as the old, shall run and sail to give to Heathendom the heavenly learning of the cross.

Another of the natural provisions for social progress is language. If men are mutually to improve each other's condition, they must have a power of expression; if one generation is to garner up its information, and bequeath its experience to posterity, it must have the power of giving its ideas not only a permanent but a communicable form. Speech and writing are these powers. They bespeak an intention that ideas should be conveyed from man to man, from community to community, from age to age. Thus wisdom is both portable and accumulated. What is newly acquired is added to an old and imperishable stock. Men die, but their thoughts, their learning, will survive. The whole race is quickened, and quickened ever freshly and progressively, by the communicative brain and heart of the surrounding and foregoing humanity. The very existence of speech and writing thus becomes a demonstration of a progressive tendency in Society. Furthermore, there is a constant advance in language itself, as to its simplicity, compass, exactness, and especially its uniformity. As civilization advances, the number of dialects decreases, provincialisms are merged, and the same tongue becomes common to all. Humboldt points out the great diversity of dialects among American savages. Sixty different vocabularies were found in Brazil alone. In Australia, there is no classifying the complexities. Among the cannibal population of Borneo, an island only eight hundred miles long, there are said to be hundreds of languages. Generally, "the number of languages in any given district is in the inverse proportion of the intellectual culture of the inhabitants." And this rule itself indicates a relation between the structure of Society and its advance from a lower to a loftier state.

It is very remarkable with what significant pro visions, with what sacred immunities, the Maker of man has guarded the principle, that by social intercommunications man shall gain his best furtherance,—by social restriction, isolation, or artificial protection, he shall wither away. Marriages of consanguinity depress or deform the vitality of the offspring. Beyond the circle of kindred, a definite localized population, that should keep on intermarrying, upon the same social grade, under the same general influences, would inevitably deteriorate. The generations need to change the air, and import unfamiliar elements. It is said that no pastoral race, a class whose range of thought is usually limited, has ever adopted a new mode of life, uninfluenced by external alliances.* To the want of renovation from without the best ethnologists attribute the barbarism that has prevailed so obstinately in Africa, in the South Sea Islands, in southern Asia. Everybody knows how the jealousy of foreign nations, as in China and Japan, has aggravated the stupidity, arrested development, stunted the national mind. To make the illustration more pertinent, the men of that portion of the Chinese people which is unquestionably the superior—the Mantchews—received their impulse from the enemies they had subdued. On the opposite side ot the planet, the aboriginal Indians of this continent roamed at will, to be sure, through the forests; but "as it were by one universal magic spell of enchantment, they kept rigidly and strictly to their respective tribes,"—oceans hemmed them in,—no people of higher civilization came in contact with them, nor, when such a people came at last, would they adopt its manners,—and "by such isolation

* W. C. Taylor's "Natural History of Society," i. 197.

through a succession of ages they have dwindled into intellectual pigmies, compared with those whose races were renovated and refreshed by the grafting of other varieties."

What goes with equal force to the same point, is the fact that in those vast peoples where there has most evidently been a decline and a deterioration from a former civilization into barbarity,—like the Peruvians, like the Copts of Egypt, like the early Greeks, like the Hindoos,—there are almost always found traditions, and sometimes relics, of the former glory, the fables of the inhabitants still referring that glory to visits of the gods,—some superior, celestial race. An examination of these fables easily satisfies us that they generally point to colonists from foreign countries, whom time and superstition have apotheosized, and invested with the attributes of divinity.

Now, if Mr. Buckle's monstrous theory were sound, that civilization is owing entirely to intellectual causes, to the exclusion of the moral, then there ought to be no such thing as a decline of civilization known on the earth. We know that the moral states of communities do vary, rising and falling at their freewill; and these States, which in our view are the grand determiners of social welfare, carry the whole commonwealth up or down with them. But leaving them out, as Mr. Buckle does, what is there to bring an eclipse over a nation's glory? Nothing short of some anomalous catastrophe,—a swoon of the national understanding, or a cataclysm in matter, obliterating at once all the attainments of the past. Herculaneum and Pompeii should be not only instances, but should fix the rule of all the ruins of peoples. What does, in fact, actually arrest social progress is moral disorder.

If the spirit of Society has one adversary more unyielding and powerful than others, it is the spirit of caste, or a privileged class. Absolute *individual* isolation is impossible. The simplest and commonest wants of our nature require a certain degree of association. The selfish principle, therefore, does not go for the hermit's cave, for the monk's cell, for Simeon's pillar. It does what is equally selfish, more convenient, and more cunning. It seeks a small and exclusive association, with a monopoly of the good things of life, in material comfort, in government, in religion; and, in that narrow beat of supercilious manners, finds a favoring theatre for pride, luxury, ambition, or sloth. This class-distinction, confined to no form of political sway, is essentially and radically anti-social. Sometimes it has organized itself, and become the accepted rule, the settled curse of the country. Where that is the case, the blight on human nature is most frightful; progress stops; enterprise is paralyzed; everything stands still perhaps for centuries. Then the laws of social activity are overborne, and held fast, in a mortmain too heavy and tight to let humanity move. And no step forward is taken, till, by some convulsion initiated from without, or brought in from above, the fatal system is broken up.

We have two definite and instructive examples in the society of Egypt and of India.

Nothing historical is better established than that at a very ancient period, as early as the reign of the Pharaohs and the age of Moses, there prevailed in Egypt a remarkably high form of civilization. Monumental inscriptions, recent explorations, allusions in the Pentateuch, references in secular chronicles, all prove that in arts and manufactures, in legislation and learning, in acquaintance with the secrets of nature and the control of her forces, the Egyptians of that time occupied the front rank of the world. This civilization afterwards declined and was lost. The nation went steadily backward. How did it happen? Does not the fact contradict our doctrine of the law of social progress? On the contrary, it signally confirms it. There grew up in

Egypt that enormous and powerful sacerdotal caste, by which the law of Society was systematically affronted. The priesthood, by craft and superstition, gradually fastened on the nation a yoke that smothered its life, infinitely more disastrous than the slavery under which the Israelites groaned when Moses, the emancipator, was born; a plague of slow effects, but finally working out social destruction. To keep all safe, in this dead-lock of the intellect and the will, foreigners were forbidden to pass the frontiers; all channels, by which new ideas could pour in to shame the stupidity or to compete with the monopoly of these self-constituted dictators, were cut off; commerce was given up to the Phœnicians, and after the days of Sesostris no effort was made to expand the state. "In religion, caste produces a tedious ceremonial and an unmeaning ritual; in politics, it creates a law fettered by usages and precedents, but destitute of the vivifying power of jurisprudence to accommodate it to times and circumstances; and in the arts of life, though it may increase the perfection of old processes, it effectually prevents new discoveries. Every one that visits a collection of Egyptian antiquities will be struck by the excellence of the manipulation, and the poverty of invention displayed in the patterns." In due time, retribution arrived.

Psammetichus, seeking assistance abroad, succeeded in dissolving the priestly caste. But it was too late; the work of death on the national spirit was too far done. His jealous warriors emigrated by thousands to Ethiopia. The offended hierocracy forsook him. The Babylonians, at Carchemish, conquered Necho, his son. Neither he, nor Hophra, his successor, could reanimate the prostrate soul of Egypt. When Amasis, a child of the people, of an inferior caste, put himself at the head of his impatient countrymen, a brief shudder of returning enterprise ran through the emasculate body of the state. But Persia bore down with her irresistible hosts; as always happens, the stronger race prevailed over the weaker; Cambyses drove the aristocratic corporation from their temples and entrenchments; "there was no room in the ancient constitution for the new elements;" "the boasted wisdom of the Egyptians became henceforth nothing more than a reminiscence and a name;" "neither the swords of the mercenaries nor the treasures of the people could uphold the throne of the Pharaohs.*

Turn to India. The great majority of that people, — according to "Ward's View of the Hindoos" about three quarters, — including all the laboring classes, — belong to the despised caste of Sudras;

* Heeren and Taylor.

while the other quarter domineer and draw up their phylacteries. Ages have not essentially altered their degraded condition. Distinctions of personal character are sunk in this flat subjection. According to the Institutes of Menu, and the accounts of Sir William Jones in his day, if a member of this outcast class presumed to take a seat by the side of his superiors, he was to be banished from the country. If he spoke of them with contempt, his mouth was to be burned; if he insulted them, his tongue was to be slit; if he sat on the same carpet with a Brahmin, he was to be maimed for life; if he listened to the reading of the sacred books, his invasion of that priestly privilege was to be rewarded by having burning oil poured into his ears; if he committed them to memory, he was to be killed; if he married his daughter to a Brahmin, no earthly vengeance was equal to the case, and he must be dismissed to infernal torments; even if his master manumitted him, he would continue a slave by nature, and never have the rights of freedom; and if murdered himself, the penalty would be only the same as for killing a cow, a dog, or a cat.

Such was the social structure of the Hindoos. More precisely to sustain the position I have already illustrated, their Brahmins adroitly forestalled the liberalizing influence of foreign intercourse, by denouncing *loss* of caste upon any one of their order who should go on a long voyage. And so the crippled Indian nation stands, or crawls, to-day, the most striking and solemn monument on earth of natural opportunities wasted, early advantages baffled, and a healthy growth of humanity arrested, by a direct denial of the ordinances by which God has appointed Society to go forward.

Just as the intellect of the individual man is ordained to be both a producer and a receiver, and to grow strong by both these activities; just as a reciprocal taking in and giving out,—inhalation and expiration,—is the law of organic life, vegetable, animal, intellectual, moral, so it is with the growth of Society; so it is with any particular local Society. The body must both receive and impart; it must eat and work; there must be respiration and perspiration. Pores and cells and senses must be open to influence,—inflowings from abroad; and, equally, sinews, limbs, powers, must be ready for action outward, from within. "So build we up our being." So, inch by inch, and bud by bud, the tree builds up its towering trunk, its pillared branches, its dome of living green. So Society builds up its more wonderful, complex organism, beneficent and beautiful. And in each and all of them, it is God that is the real Builder,—the "wise master-builder,"—working ever, through alternate regularity and variation, that thing which is best, by his own divine and perfect law.

The preparations for this mutual process are laid, fast and fruitful, in our social nature. By both propensities man is ever pushed toward his fellow-man,—by the desire to gain from him, by the desire to impart to him. Hence intercourse, instruction, commerce, travel, colonization. Thereby different communities, as villages, cities, tribes, nations, extend and flourish. In proportion as the social propensity has room to play itself out into action, gets air and light, the people prospers. Shut it up to itself, and it is starved and dwindled. As to all the grand objects of a noble commonwealth, insulate it and it pines away, gasping for the breath of life.

Surveying social history, to see how its strongest movements have sprung up, where its most rapid advancements have been achieved, where the seats of its intensest energy have been planted, you will see this law everywhere fulfilled. Where social communications have been freest, civilization has ripened fastest. Interchange has been inspiration. Mixtures of bloods have been parents of progress and power. Contact of humanity with humanity has been like the touch of the prophet's bones; it has made the dead start up alive. It is the true Promethean fire, running from country to country, leaping from heart to heart, passed in lamps and torches from hand to hand as they meet,* animating, brightening, gladdening the world. It never poisons nor palsies those that take it, nor binds them on a rock, nor eats out their vitals. It emancipates them rather from the bondage of their barbarism, and from the vultures of ignorance, superstition and sloth.

It was when the eastern tribes began to stir and intermix, that ideas began to take the place of mere physical necessities, in controlling human life. The shocks of nation against nation woke up the intellect from its lethargy, and struck out vastly more of discovery, of thought, of original force, than would have come from a mere addition of the several amounts. It was not a process of addition but of multiplication. As, in certain chemical combinations, you get not only the aggregate of the substances you throw in, but new qualities, finer forces, or fairer forms, by their chemical action, so in the great crucible of a continent, when you pour the currents of national life together, by

* Λαμπάδια ἔχοντες διαδώσουσιν ἀλλήλοις.

certain secret forces of assimilation and repulsion higher institutions, better forms of civilized society, appear. In his eloquent and very instructive work on "The Earth and Man," Professor Guyot has so ably handled and exhausted the whole subject of the divine adaptation and relation between the physical and the moral creation, that if I were to transfer to my argument his ninth and twelfth lectures entire, I should only strengthen and adorn it. There we see how the shapings of the continents, the expanses of the ocean, the courses of rivers and the configurations of hills are exactly contrived to favor and to consummate just that social result which we have all along found indicated as God's design in Society itself, viz., unity in the midst of diversity,—a common spirit widened and deepened by individual peculiarity and liberty. There we see Asia, Europe, North America, as the three grand stages in the march of civilization. There we see the great silent, swinging globe itself, moving, stirring, impelling, shaking together, and compacting again, into an ultimate order of inconceivable magnitude and glory, from the East and from the West, from the North and from the South, the children of God that walk, and work, and suffer, and think, and weep, and pray, on its breast. Hence it was,—from this geographic preparation,—that the chief developments of human enterprise and ingenuity so long took place about the eastern extremity of the Mediterranean. There, as Napoleon said, the human soul throbbed most powerfully. There all the natural conditions of prosperous life were best fulfilled and combined,—a soft climate, various lands, spontaneous and nutritious productions, so that, *up to a certain point*,—that point, viz., where a greater degree of hardihood becomes necessary to complete manhood, Society was left free for its most favorable manifestations, while the rude navigation of those waters was a constant stimulant to the communities around it. Later, when this Mediterranean civilization had done its best, and its several members,—Phœnicia, Egypt, Tyre, Greece, Italy, Spain, Carthage,—had done all for each other that they could do,—how was the next great step forward to be taken? Providence answered, by bringing down a new element from the North; a rough bridegroom from the forest for this southern bride. To be sure, it was a wild wooing, and a fiercer wedlock; but nevertheless the marriage was pronounced; the domestic doors of Europe were opened; the nations mixed; God's designs went forward. With their *quick, bold faculties, Goths, Vandals, Franks*, adopted whatever was best in the life of the countries they conquered. Then the scene of human activity was shifted to another theatre, further west. Germany, France, Great Britain, and Italy, by their action and interaction, strife and treaty, stimulus and competition, took up and bore forward the ameliorations of the world. Arts, sciences, printing, and a wider commerce, were finally born. And by commerce, later yet, just when a larger scope was wanted, the veil was lifted before a more magnificent theatre still. Not now a union of the nations of a continent, but of continents themselves! Columbus came. America was found. The new career began of that admixture, on a scale of unprecedented grandeur, of which the ultimate results, after three centuries and a half, lie still unforeseen, unimagined, undreamed in the future.

From one point in the interior of Asia, little more than a dot on the rind of the globe, the waves of advancing civilization steadily spread. They crept slowly to the Mediterranean. The Persian power gave the human tide a new impulse and sent it to the Ægean. The Greeks bore it forward to the Adriatic. The Romans pressed it on to the Atlantic. There it rested long, baffled by the waste sea, till, in the fulness of time, God put the freight of an old world's hope into the fragile fleet of a Genoese sailor and floated it to the new. Two formidable ramparts of mountains, and as many thousands of miles, are conquered in three centuries more. Then California launches for China. The Pacific,—name of prophecy and promise,—ocean of the world's final peace,—is crossed. The colonizing of the Pacific islands completes the chain. Diffusion first, then assimilation. First the genius of Progress peoples the earth. Then she returns on her track, resets, in better symmetry, the growths she had planted, and makes the expanded household one. Dispersion is a civilizer; and so is centralization; each in turn; each counterpoised by the other. "Give me the map of a country," says Cousin, "its configuration, its climate, its waters, its winds, its natural productions, its botany, its zoology, and all its physical geography, and I pledge myself to tell you what will be the man of this country, and what place this country will occupy in history."

If finer specimens of our kind, and loftier degrees of civilization, are to be developed on this hemisphere than ever before, it will be because here the people of all the nations on the earth meet each other on more liberal terms, and enter into less obstructed alliances; because no narrow national policy bars any out, and no oppression of government enslaves any after they are in; because all bring their gifts, their traditions, their faculties, their blood, their hopes, their faiths, and fusing them all together, doubtless through many a collision uncomfortable to taste and awkward to prejudice,—yet under the benign and foreseeing Providence ot the Father of them all, work out, and rear peacefully together such a Christian commonwealth of mind and heart and conscience and will, of beauty and strength, of law and love, as the sun never beheld.*

Peacefully; you mark that word; and you say it suggests a painful commentary. For, very often, these mixtures of peoples have been effected only through fire and sword, through campaigns, sieges, slaughters. Can these be social agencies? Are they not anti-social rather, springing from hate, not love? Is war ever a civilizer?

The answer to these questions cannot be put into a single word. If men had been ready and equal to the progressive plans of Providence,—if those plans took no resistance nor contravention from mortal passions, mortal sluggishness, or selfishness, I suppose the social mixtures I have referred to would be effected without hostile collisions. Our

* Hegel supposes the logical end of human history to be on the continent of Europe,—probably in Prussia.

presumptions, in such a field of speculation, ought, of course, to be modest. But it seems at least reasonable to suppose that in that case, the steady march of improvement would be no march of armed hosts, with bloody hands; the horrible arts and machinery of destruction would be displaced by industry and friendly traffic; countries would open their gates to each other, learn war no more, and thrive, as they ultimately will, surely as God lives, on one another's prosperity. And yet, notwithstanding the obvious incongruity between bloodshed and a spirit of social progress, by looking further down, we shall discover a certain philosophical and real relation between them. Taking men as they are, with all their deformities, and weaknesses, and ignorances, wars have come about, in the accomplishment of the same ends which would have been accomplished otherwise had men been what they ought to be. The social instinct has pushed men on, to meet each other, and occupy the globe. Encountering opposition, they have fought. With what was natural and providential in these instincts, self-interest and violence have profusely mingled. Yet even then, how often has the overruling hand of God come in to turn the warrior and destroyer into servants of his will, to make the wrath and the policy and the powder of man to praise him, to gather from the field of havoc some harvest of human welfare afterwards,— as the sweet, yellow grain waves every summer on the acres of Waterloo. The military occupation of the Scottish Highlands, after the battle of Culloden, was an advantage to that rude region which can be traced in all its subsequent condition. Following almost every great war, there has been a new impulse to human progress. Old conventions and abuses were broken up; old prejudices, superstitions, dynasties were sundered; old chains were snapped to pieces. Nations burst through their former boundaries; they crossed their blood; they sharpened their brains; they liberalized their judgments; they enlarged their experience. A fresh start, though often a short and interrupted one, was given to the general advance. The actors in the struggle may have been rapacious, cruel, infamous. They followed a horrid and accursed trade. But if all the evil was man's, all the final good was God's; and the last and greatest victory is always the victory of his love.

So, friends, the Almighty Providence, which never sleeps, draws his children on. And where he draws, it is no aimless movement. We see but the surface, — or only margins and glimpses of the mighty plan. All the revolutions of our latest times are only the breaking crests of a wave of light that has been rolling on, ever since God divided the ocean from the land, the morning from the night. The world is not a self-impelled caprice. History is not a tangled skein. Civilization is not scattered by chance, but grows by law. We call single events, or lordly men, the causes of great epochs. But the causes lie deeper and act further than single events or the lordliest men. They are bedded deep by the Creator in the bosom of Humanity. They act through long reaches of social succession. Moses, inspired prophet as he was, did not rear the Hebrew commonwealth, nor emancipate Israel; but He who said to Moses, "The I AM hath sent thee." "The Roman republic was overthrown, not by Cæsar and Pompey, but by that condition of things which made Cæsar and Pompey possible." Luther, Calvin and Zuingle did not reform Europe, and transform the Church, but He, the Church's Head, their Lord and Master, who said once, and says forever, "If the Truth shall make you free, ye shall be free indeed." Washington and the immortal signers of the Declaration did not create American independence, nor drive back the troops of the Crown, but that Arm that overturns and delivers, that pulleth down one, and setteth up another.

Down through all that mingled play of the evil and the good that have made up the fortunes of the world, there has run the adamantine chain of a heavenly Design. Its first link is held by the hand of a personal God; and however dim our eyes may be in tracing out its windings, yet, when all shall be unfolded at last, faith tells us that it will end where it began; that the last link shall lie firmly, with the first, in the same Father's hand, binding all in one, and all to Him.

As with construction, so with retribution. When the crime and selfishness of empires stop the coming of the Son of Man too long, and humanity falls helpless among thieves and robbers, and oppression heaps its insults in the face of Heaven's anointed, then the same law that went forth once from Jerusalem comes in justice again. Again you see the hand-writing of the fingers on the walls of tyranny, and hear the footsteps of the Avenger. Then the awful Presence, from which nothing hides, moves in among corrupted courts, or guilty senates, or cabinets that sell man and truth for gold. Then, by the direct and irresistible working of the social laws, commercial robbery, the monopolies of wealth, or Corinthian manners, prepare and inflict for themselves Heaven's merciful revenge. Then what conformity had disordered, reform, with a face of terror, and hands of iron that break in pieces, yet with a heart of compassion, comes to purify and to heal. And though venerable and beautiful forms are shattered, it is to liberate a spirit imprisoned in them, more venerable, more beautiful, because more useful still.

"Young Romance raised his dreamy eyes,
O'erhung with dainty locks of gold;
Why smite, he asked, in sad surprise,
The fair, the old?

"Yet louder rang the strong one's stroke,
Yet nearer flashed his axe's gleam;
Shuddering and sick at heart I woke,
As from a dream.

"I looked: aside the dust-cloud rolled;
The waster seemed the builder too;—
Upspringing from the ruined Old
I saw the New.

"'T was but the ruin of the bad,—
The wasting of the wrong and ill;
Whate'er of good the old time had
Was living still.

"Calm grew the brow of him I feared;
The frown which awed me passed away,
And left behind a smile that cheered
Like breaking day.

"The grass grew green on battle-plains,
O'er swarded war-mounds grazed the cow;
The slave stood forging, from his chains,
The spade and plough."

"Thus the gazers of the nations, and the watchers of the skies,
Looking through the coming ages, shall behold, with joyful eyes,
On the fiery track of Freedom fall the mild baptismal rain,
And the ashes of old evil feed the Future's golden grain."

LECTURE VIII.

SOCIETY THE SPHERE OF THE KINGDOM OF CHRIST ON EARTH.

THE first announcement of Christianity to the world contained in it a promise of a new order of Society. When the Divine Person that embodied and proclaimed this religion came forward, out of the retirements of Nazareth, to his public ministry, he came not only as the Regenerator and Redeemer of the individual heart, but as a Recreator of social institutions and the Saviour of states. Earlier yet, the anticipations of prophecy had described him as the Author of a commonwealth complete in compass, power, harmony, every civic glory. The imagery that pictured that foreseen splendor was drawn from social reconciliations, swords beaten into ploughshares, Ethiopia stretching out her hands, the wolf lying down with the lamb, tyranny and hatred vanished from the family of nations. In these generous predictions we hear the mighty forechant of that universal anthem which is to rise from all the round world, Christianized and consecrated at last. The Messiah expected was to be a Prince of unbroken peace, and of his brotherly kingdom there should be no end.

At his actual coming, these animating and benignant promises were more than confirmed. The first voice that declared his nativity,—ringing through the midnight sky over Bethlehem,—the celestial chorus startling the shepherds,—was a song of hope for social man, as well as a "Gloria in Excelsis" to the Creator; for, after its first sublime ascription to Heaven, comes instantly the "Peace on earth, good will to men." Every supernatural sign spoke of human reformation. The Advent was a coming of the Son of God to weary, oppressed, sorrowing humanity. The Epiphany was a manifestation of the Father to an alienated, scattered household. The Passion was a redemptive suffering for a bleeding social body, no less than for lost solitary souls. Throughout all his benign ministry, Christ planted virtues which are the very binding and healing and building of the social state. With the clearest emphasis he affirmed that his mission was to rear a world-wide home for the tribes of the earth,—under one Father and one law,—"that they all might be one." To this purified and Christian society he gave a social name—the Church. Its organizing principle was to be the spirit of his own life and gospel, wrought first into the convictions and thus into the whole development and conformation of the race.

The reach of time it will require to work this consummation out is never estimated. The uncertain and variable element is the freewill of man; the element fixed and sure is the decree of God. All we know of the period of the plan is that it is His with whom one day is as a thousand years. Whenever the result is accomplished, it will doubtless be through the voluntary consent of men themselves, who are to be the material as well as the architects of the structure. In my last Lecture I endeavored to show that though the rate is not uniform, nor the progress equal as to place, the causes that shall finally work that Christian commonwealth into realization, act steadily and unceasingly, from age to age, with the constancy and the power of law.

Now the means by which this grand, ultimate destiny of mankind is to be achieved, we know. It is by the ideas and affections, *i. e.*, by the spiritual forces,—planted germinally by the Creator in humanity, and manifested perfectly in the one Divine Man. In history we know them as Life; in the gospel as Truth. What we name Christianity is the clear and complete affirmation of them by that mediatorial Being, in his action, in his speech, in his death, in his resurrection, in the eternal intercessory and inspiring office of his Lordship in the heavens. Thus the social constitution of man, and the revelation in Christ, are the two correlated, complemental forces, which bear forward the progress of the world. Together, they prepare that renewed, just, free, merciful and holy society which the New Testament repeatedly characterizes as the kingdom of heaven on earth, and which is the symbol, the archetype, and the beginning of that final and everlasting kingdom which *shall be* when there shall be new heavens and a new earth. This, in as few terms as I am able to present it, is the key to the Christian philosophy of history.

It follows that when the great truths of Christianity shall have become embodied in the actual forms of government, education, trade, art, letters, mercy, manners and worship, and shall have controlled Society by their living power, then the kingdom of Christ will have come. Whether this result is ever to be an historical fact on this planet, *i. e.*, whether the human race is literally perfectible,—or whether, in a state meant to be disciplinary and preparatory, it shall be realized only in approximate and ever-ascending degrees, is not important to the integrity of our reasoning. It is enough if all the currents of history stream that way, and if both the tendencies and aspirations of men point and climb ever to the same zenith of the future. It is the distinctively Christian element of this view which distinguishes it from an atheistic theory like that of Auguste Comte, who would make the three great eras of perfected humanity to be the Metaphysical, the Theological and the Scientific, and would subordinate religion to "positive knowledge:" on the other hand, it is its comprehensive character, as embracing all of Christendom, which distinguishes it from the limited conceptions of Christian writers like Bossuet and Schlegel, who would confine all possible progress to the Roman Catholic communion.

The position taken is this: It is through men's social relations and affections, that Christ, the Head of the race, proposes to construct his spiritual empire, his church. What we name history is only the unrolling of the scenes of that construction. Old Thomas Fuller is justified in saying that of the four proper aims of the historian, the first is the glory of God. For what this reverent scholar would place first in the writing of history, God himself has plainly put first in the history to be written. Even Montesquieu, who in an earlier work* spoke lightly of Christianity, after experience had matured his mind acknowledged that it was not only the most perfect form of religion, but the principal "support of the social system."

Men may dispute whether there was a golden age in the Past, but there shall be a true golden age before us: prophecy foretells it; hope reaches toward it; experience opens her secret pledges of it; all the voices of heaven and earth promise it; and imagination has only to bring her pencil of brilliant light to picture its scenery of majesty and splendor: a period, in the slightly altered and beautiful language of Coleridge, "when conscience shall act in man with the ease and uniformity of instinct; when labor shall be a sweet name for the activity of sane minds in healthful bodies, and all enjoy in common the bounteous harvest produced by common effort: when there shall exist in the sexes, and in the individuals of each sex, just variety enough to call forth the gentle restlessness and final union of chaste love and individual attainment, each seeking and finding the beloved one by the natural affinity of their beings; when the Sovereign of the universe shall be known only as the universal Parent,—no altar but

* *Lettres Persanes.*

the pure heart, and thanksgiving and grateful love the sole sacrifice."

"Then comes the statelier Eden back to men;
Then reign the world's great bridals, chaste and calm;
Then springs the crowning race of human kind."

Such a result can stand second to no other in the purposes of God for mankind. If Society is the proper and pre-adapted theatre for the embodiment and the free working out of the vital ideas of Christianity, then no other proof can be brought forward, so clear and so decisive, that Society is a practical illustration of the Power, and the Wisdom, and the Goodness of God. For these ideas are the very hiding of his Power, and the Light of his Wisdom; the human souls they fill and actuate are the very children of his Fatherhood, the joy of his infinite heart of love.

As I shall arrange and mention them, these ideas are seven: 1. The Historic Unity of Mankind. 2. Dependent Trust, or Faith. 3. Moral Rectitude. 4. Charity. 5. Obedience. 6. The Balance of Conservatism and Reform. 7. Voluntary Sacrifice.

I. Society is the appointed sphere of the spiritual kingdom of Christ, because a moral and organic unity embraces its parts and links together its successive generations. Were there no such law of transmission, no chain of connection between age and age, no hereditary conveyance of moral qualities, then it is evident Christianity could get no leverage, and no grasp on the world's motives. We could not speak of the building of a kingdom, or the unfolding of a method of progression. Each rank of souls must then begin at the same starting-place, and drop at the same goal. The operation of Christian Truth on the ages would be only a monotonous repetition of the same unfinished experiment, ever begun with the birth, ever broken off with the death, of the individual.

It requires only a moderate study of the actual operation of Christian truth around us every day to see how the hereditary relations are taken up and made use of as an effectual remedial agency to recover men from their evils. If souls fall out of the way by these connections when they are vitiated, so are they manifestly restored by them when they are sanctified. This line of thought has been very ingeniously and eloquently pursued by a writer of our own day,* who asks, "What intelligent person ever supposed that this original constitution, by which one generation derives its existence and receives the bent of its character from

* Rev. Horace Bushnell, D.D., in "Christian Nurture."

another, was designed of God to be the vehicle only of depravity? The only supposition that honors God is that the organic unity was ordained originally for the nurture of holy virtue in the beginning of each soul's history; and that Christianity, or redemption, must of necessity take possession of the abused vehicle, and sanctify it for its own merciful uses."

In the language of another, "Philosophy ever contemplates man as a concrete,—humanity entire in its unity. Experience, with its broadest inductions, confirms the existence of a law above that which reigns in the individual, and which binds all individuals in one community. The perpetuation of the characteristic human form, and mental faculty, and relative proportion of sex, and the one consecutive stream of historic development for men, all evince that there is a persistent causality, before and above all individual peculiarity." It is plain that only on such a law of unity in the race, and out of its practical energy, could there be planted and reared a social institution, ever advancing to the realization of a heavenly ideal, like the Christian church. "An unbroken and real spiritual chain of instruction, example, influence, fellowship, connects Abraham, the 'father of the faithful,' with the lastest generation that shall walk in the footsteps of his faith,—the cradle of the Church in the tent of Mamre, and its school-days in the temple at Jerusalem, with the widest and most spiritual triumphs of its maturity."

Hence the secret current of transmitted and generative life, in the order of successive spiritual dispensations,—each an outgrowth of the foregoing, —each prophesying and preparing its successor. The biblical dispensations are three,—types of three great principles of moral action,—three stages in the religious discipline of Society: the Patriarchal, the Mosaic, the Christian; impulse, law, love; nature, government, grace; instinct, obedience, faith; Mamre, Sinai, Calvary. This is the order. Natural impulse, when the parental arm is not pressed around it, runs wild, and needs the restraining hand of law. Moses comes with his commandments, ordinances, ritual, and manifold rules and ceremonies, to yoke the wayward will in obedience, —an age of legality. Afterwards, in the fulness of time, when the schoolmaster has done his work, when man by obeying has grown to the liberty of choice, when, by being a servant under the commandment, he has learned the faith to which grace can safely speak, then appears the Messiah: the Desire of all nations,—He that was to come,—the great Reality of all the symbols. Adam and

Christ are thus the two poles of history. "The first Adam was made a living soul; the second Adam was the Lord from heaven." First, a natural creation, and an outward culture. Then a spiritual creation, and a regeneration from within,—Christ formed in the heart. This is for Society just as truly as for the individual; historical no less than personal. It is the whole procession of the centuries that strews the palm branches in the way for the Saviour. The kingdom of the Son of Man, in the future, is established on all the experience of the humanity that has gone before. And from the fair beginnings in the elder Eden, we look to the sublime redemptive consummation in that other Paradise that is to spring up on the earth, yet so beautiful that it shall seem to descend, like a bride, out of heaven.

Nay, if we take our stand with the Scotch philosopher, who joins faith with science,* we shall descry the preparations of this final harmony of the social and the evangelical systems far back before the first man breathed, and catch the notes of the august prelude among the inarticulate sounds and motions of the pre-Adamic creation. "In the history of the earth which we inhabit," he says, "molluscs, fishes, reptiles, mammals, had, each in

* Hugh Miller.

succession, their periods of vast duration, and then the human period began,—the period of a fellow-worker with God, created in God's own image. What is to be the next advance? Is there to be merely a repetition of the Past? No. The geologist, in those tables of stone which form his records, finds no example of epochs, once passed away, again returning. There has been no repetition of the dynasty of the fish, of the reptile, of the mammal. The dynasty of the future is to have glorified man for its inhabitant; but it is to be the dynasty,—'the kingdom,'—not any longer of man made in the image of God, but of God himself in the form of man. There we find the point of elevation, never to be exceeded, meetly coincident with the final period, never to be terminated,—the infinite in height harmoniously associated with the eternal in duration. Creation and the Creator meet at one point, and in one person. The long ascending line from dead matter to man has been a progress Godwards,—not an asymptotical progress, but destined, from the beginning, to furnish a point of union of man with his Maker. Like the Patriarchal and Mosaic dispensations of grace, the Palæozoic, the Secondary and the Tertiary dispensations of creation were charged with 'the shadows of better things to come.' The advent of man, simply as such, was the great event prefigured during the old geologic ages. The advent of that divine Man, who hath abolished death and brought life and immortality to light, was the great event prefigured during the historic ages. It is these two grand events, equally portions of one sublime scheme, that bind together Past, Present and Future, the geologic with the Patriarchal, Mosaic and Christian ages, and all together with the new heavens, the last of many creations, when there shall be no more death nor curse, but the throne of God and the Lamb shall be in it, and his servants shall serve him."

II. The second of these primary ideas of Christianity is Dependence,—with its correlative sentiment, Faith. Sooner or later, man has to learn that he is weak, and with a weakness that does not necessarily degrade but is meant finally to educate and exalt him. He has to learn that he must lean upon the Power, and be guided by the Wisdom, and be nourished by the Goodness, that is far, far above him. He is but a child in the temple, crying, "Lord, here am I; speak, for thy servant heareth." He is but a suppliant asking alms at the temple-gate of the abundant Providence. He is but the blind pilgrim of a wide sea, —tempest and darkness riding the waters with him, and only one unseen hand to make a safe path over the deep. Pain and sickness, the swaddling bands of the cradle and the shroud with which others' hands gird him, calamity and death, accident and the frailties of age,—all these are the stern preceptors and the sombre symbols of that dependence. Till he feels it as a fact, till he confesses it as a blessing, till he rejoices gratefully in it as a religious bond pressing him ever back closer and closer to the Fatherly Breast where his life is hid, he is only an exile from his country, and an orphan in his house.

The whole frame of Society is a nursery for that faith. It is a network of dependencies, of weak upon strong, of poor upon affluent, and not less of the slender rich upon the laboring poor,—of young upon old, of posterity upon ancestry, of class upon class, of city and country on each other, of subject upon ruler, of debtor upon creditor, of enterprise upon combination, of every member upon the social system he lives in. Helpless we are born into parental arms, and lie dependent there. Helpless, with our maturest strength and readiest wit, we reach out our faculties towards other persons, to hold by them, and live from them. Helpless we grow old, and tremble toward our graves, that some gentle reverence and love may come, and uphold, and wait for, and forbear with us. By these natural leanings we may learn our heavenly lesson. They are the alphabet of our immortal trust. Reposing in arms that shall crumble one day to dust, we come to feel how an Arm that is never shortened and never wastes is under us. When the Master says, "Have faith in God," or "Thy faith hath saved thee," our tender human relationships have interpreted the precept and reëcho the assurance; and when his apostle writes, "With the heart man believeth," or "Faith is the evidence of things not seen," sweet motherly faces, noble and manly foreheads, men we have known, of unassailable truth and honor, or women whose constancy finds no likeness in sun or star — yes, the motherhood we have nestled under or the manhood we have clung to,—throng up for our witnesses that it is true; till, turning back from the dependencies of earth to that Arm which never changes in the skies, we answer in earnest, "Lord, I believe; help thou mine unbelief!" The social system is thus a nursery for religious dependence and faith.

III. Next, we must remember that Christianity is a system not only of spiritual affections but of moral duties; and to these moral duties Society is essential. Indeed, they could have exercise nowhere else but in its reciprocal relationships, of the family, the neighborhood, traffic, politics, education, charity. Morality is the right dealing of man with man,—necessarily a social obligation. So of all its several branches, which we call virtues, but which are in fact only so many shoots of one great stock of virtue,—the loyal love of the Right. Take justice: where can it get such a discipline as where social causes constantly create the temptation indeed to defraud, to overreach, to injure, in dealings, in competitions, in slanderous speech, yet where the social welfare is ever clearly seen to stand exactly accordant with the precept, "Render to every man that which is just and equal?" Take veracity: the social world, with its conflict of selfish and generous passions, you say, is a tremendous nursery of falsehood; but precisely in the degree it is so, it reveals the glory, and measures the value, of that simple and valiant tongue of truth, without which all social peace sinks in treachery and despair. Take purity: it is only through the mixtures, solicitations and stimulants of social scenes that we learn the meaning of that holy beatitude, falling forever from the Mount: "Blessed are the pure in heart, for they shall see God." Take patience: how should we ever learn to forbear, and forgive, and conquer petulance, and be still, if, all the way, life through, child with child in the nursery, disease with health, differing temperaments with each other, partners in business, wedded pairs, unlike tastes and habits and cultures and tempers all tossed and huddled together,—we did not find out by vexing lessons how wonderful is the patience of God? I confess, the longer I live, no attribute of his awes me so much. Take fortitude: and for every hero that bravely adventures against nature, and conquers polar ice, or vanquishes the ominous terrors of spectral fears, I will show you a grander heroism, a loftier, mightier courage, in the youth that dares to do right in the boarding-school, in the young girl that dares to be simple in the evening assembly, in the woman that dares to be independent of the despotism and sin of fashion, in the man that dares to be righteous, against his party, his promotion, or his pocket. Here are the trial-places of the Christian moralities. It is a terrible ordeal. But except it were a trial, a choice, and a battle, there would be no morals that Christ would accept. And the same social world that plies the discipline, presents also the motive, and points ever to the animating reward, in that purified social condition of which the kingdom of Christ is the name.

IV. Another of the cardinal ideas of the Christian kingdom is disinterested charity. Christ came into the world to move men to love, to help, to serve each other. He came washing poor men's feet, sitting down with outcasts, dropping his benediction with the widow's mite. So wherever his religion has gone, mercy has been one of its foremost offices, and has been a test of its sincerity. "If a man love not his brother whom he hath seen, how can he love God whom he hath not seen?" The rude old European kings made the high almoner the first ecclesiastical dignitary in their dominions, and took the sacrament from his hands. The offertory became as necessary a part of the ritual as the eucharist. We call the poor Christ's poor; and we know that to neglect them is to deny him.

And evidently man is charitable because he is first social. The sphere of this Christian love can be no other than the sphere of man's social sympathies. The grand law of gospel charity was first dimly written in the constitution of Society. But what Society so deeply needs, only the motives of Christian faith can sustain. Paganism, if it cared for the poor at all, was prompted only by fickle impulse or a calculating policy. Christianity encourages the poor, lifts them out of their disabilities, and reassures their better energies, — first of all because it sees in every one of them the germ of a spiritual and immortal life. So alms-giving is transfigured into beneficence. Wise help takes the place of impulsive bounty. Paupers are made workers. Christian self-sacrifice is too real and too patient to scatter largesses, and go complacently on its way. The love of man grows out of the same root with the love of God; Brotherhood here out of the Fatherhood there. The only sustainer of philanthropy is piety. In many and many a holy enterprise of quiet compassion, throughout Christendom, we find just that to be true which is related of a hospital of Sisters of Charity, for the most wretched and vile of bed-ridden paupers in the Old World, where the religious women who ministered to the miserable inmates confessed that their only refuge from utter discouragement, in duties so revolting, even after being years in the holy work, was, by a special exercise of united prayer, every morning, to dedicate themselves anew to their task, "for the love of God." So that in all those deeds of benevolence which bless degradation, and are ever redeeming the want which still clings to the robes of the Church, Society and Christianity are expressly fitted to each other.

V. Another of the cardinal principles of Christianity is obedience, or, more exactly, a balance of personal liberty and law. That is but a soft and sentimental moral system which excludes from its circle of forces the awful energy of law. It is only when we attribute to the lawgiver, or commander, some touch of mortal imperfection, some taint of caprice or selfishness, some despotic disposition, some belittleing limitation, that we are obliged to associate servility with obedience. Let the character of the master be faultless and spotless, — nay, gathering into itself all the energies of rectitude, and all the graces of affection, and all the breadths and depths of knowledge,—in a word, let him be God,—and then obedience rises at once to moral dignity, and we see that there are no grand, proportioned, enduring, sinewy souls without it. It is only they who have been schooled somewhere to obey, that are "fit to command." Obedience breeds some of the noblest traits we ever see in the loftiest spirits. Do not confound it with fear. Obedience may spring from veneration, from thoughtfulness, from love, — the highest of all sentiments. God is the perfect Good, living. Obedience to him is one form of gratitude,—which is always the brother of magnanimity. God is better to every man than any man ever was to himself. Therefore, says Christianity, thou shalt keep the commandments of the Lord thy God.

But now, Society stands with this principle of obedience for one of its chief pillars. The doctrine of "no master, no law, no command," is anarchy, and has been, ever since time began. Human Society is a tuition in law, very faulty because its legislators are fallible, very fluctuating because all its rulers are men. But, nevertheless, everywhere, God honors it as the agent of order, and accepts its honest attempt. Indeed, it may be said the great object of social history is to find out what, or who sought to be obeyed, and thus gradually to transfer obedience from the undeserving to the worthy. The writer who maintains* that the objects of government are only temporary, and that government itself is only a proof of remaining barbarism, first confuses thought, and then abuses language. Our obedience begins with our first conscious motives,—except where parentage is faithless and abnegates its trust;—it lasts on to the final breath, except where rebel passions raise an insurrectionary signal on the way. The nursery, the house, the debating club, the shop, the office, the school, the university, the army, the farm, the professions, all are girt about by law, and subsist

* Herbert Spencer's "Social Statics."

in obedience. Ofttimes this obedience is one of the most voluntary and spontaneous acts of our souls, and then it is nearest its perfection. Then you have got for your commander, or master, the loved and trusted man. That is the happy society. Some human form, blending the honors of virtue with the sanctities of years, looks upon you with the benignant aspect of a wise, serene soul, and commands your instantaneous allegiance. Some benefactor, or lover, or hero of your private admiration, makes his choice known, and instantly friendship rears a throne of authority in the centre of your heart, and you are constrained as effectually as by any constable's staff, or cord about your wrists. *In all its sacred constitution,* Society preaches the sacredness of law, and so points, with reverent finger, from human law to the divine, and to him in whose bosom both have their seat at last. By being servants we become children and heirs. By law we gain liberty. By waiting at the foot of Sinai, we are taken up into Olivet and Tabor. The tables of stone lean against the cross. Moses is followed by the Messiah. Beyond the valleys of Subjection rise the eternal hills of Peace. The years of unquestioning and obedient toil ended, there is proclaimed the great Sabbatic festival,—where law is love, and order is choice, and government is Fatherhood, and the Ruler's will is the impulse of every heart.

Throughout these discussions of the constitution of Society, we have seen one great principle running through its activities, underlying all its forms, reappearing in all its epochs, promoted by all its development: this, viz., that the liberty and power of the individual will are meant to be held in even and perfect balance with the common good. On the one side, individual man,—his freedom and his rights sacredly guarded from infringement: on the other side, association of strength, and community of heart, never to be broken or invaded by personal selfishness or interest. In the final adjustment of these two ideas will be the harmony of the world. Over their ultimate reconciliation will be lifted the sublimest anthem ever sung since that chorus over the birth at Bethlehem.

Now it is precisely these two ideas, and precisely the practical principle of their reconciliation, that Christianity proposes, preaches and prepares. In those poised and balanced doctrines of its apostle we find this compendiously given: "Every man shall bear his own burden." "Bear ye one another's burdens, and so fulfil the law of Christ." Said the Master himself: "Except a man be born again, he shall not enter into the kingdom of heaven," — and, "Behold, a new commandment I give unto you, that ye love one another." The individualizing principle ultimates in personal character. Need I tell you that Christianity everywhere insists on that,—labors for it, exhorts to it, and brings the whole cluster of its energetic forces and doctrines to achieve it,—the regeneration, the redemption, the growth, the edifying of individual character, — its whole body fitly framed together by that which every joint supplieth. The social principle, on the contrary, signalizes itself in some form of civil law. Not less does Christianity recognize and sanction that. It honors government. It prizes order. It loves instituted right. It bids us obey the magistrate and respect the rule. And it does each for each. It keeps law sacred for the individual; it nurtures the individual for the brotherhood. Thus the laws of Society and the kingdom of Christ exactly and beautifully agree.

Sometimes, however, there comes a crisis where the strong individual conviction of Right overrides every form of human law. That is the period of revolution and reformation. It comes because the statutes of a people are only a proximate, and never yet a perfect, expression of the highest conscience of Society. It comes because, in some quick-sighted and half-inspired soul, the true sense of what is really best and really right transcends all the behests of mortal regulation and all the penalties of the statute book. It comes because deep down, in the inmost heart of his chosen children, God has written a Law which such men put higher than any law of man's making, and because they know that it is only in obedience to the Law higher than governments or states, that the government of any state, or the welfare of any people, is safe. It comes because Christ himself comes, and the Holy Spirit has not forsaken humanity. New sunrises of light and liberty come with it. Then wrong is discrowned, and error is beaten down, and the oppressed go free. Then heroes of a heavenly commission put the clarion to their lips, and the walls of a hierarchy, or of slavery, or of tyranny, are shaken down. Those are the solemn passovers of human history,—turned afterwards into jubilees, kept by grateful generations whom the sacrifice set free. The martyr dies, on his scaffold or his cross; the letter of the old law killeth him; it has just energy enough for that murder; precedent, rule, routine, law, crucify him. But the spirit of Society, when the eternal Love breathes into it, buries his body in peace, builds a monument to his brave, truthful name, and, better yet, lives out his glorious thought.

There is an incident in Italian history which so exactly illustrates this sudden outburst of irrepressible individual inspiration, breaking over the best meant law, in one single thrilling incident, that I cannot help quoting it into the argument.*

When the great obelisk brought from Egypt was erected by Fontana in the square of St. Peter's, in 1586, it was determined to make that gigantic undertaking an incarnation of the knowledge and resources of Rome. They arranged their tackle, and spotted their hands, for the delicate and perilous work. To make all safe, and prevent the possibility of accident from some sudden cry, or alarm, a papal edict was proclaimed by Sixtus V., promising death to any man who should utter a loud word till the engineer gave the signal that all risk was past. As the majestic monolithe moved up, the populace closed in; the square was crowded with admiring eyes and beating hearts. Slowly that huge crystallization of Egyptian sweat, —fit emblem of the toil-wrought column of a civilized state,—rose on its basis;—five degrees, ten, fifteen, twenty; ah, there are signs of faltering. No matter; no voice; silence; it moves again;—twenty-five, thirty, forty, forty-three; it stops; now

* The passage is taken in substance and much of the language from a lecture by Horatio Greenough.

there is trouble. Lo, those hempen cables, that like faithful servants have obeyed the mathematician, have suddenly lugged out an order from God, not to hold that base steady any longer on those terms. The engineer, who knew the hand-writing of that order, trembled. The obedient masons looked at each other, silent, and then watched the threatening, hanging mass of stone. The unspoken question was, Which way would it fall? Among the crowd, silence; silence everywhere; obedience to the law; and the sun poured down on the stillness and the despair. Suddenly, from out that breathless mass of men, rang a cry, clear as the archangel's trumpet, "*Wet the ropes!*" The crowd turned to look. Tiptoe on a post, in a jacket of homespun, his eyes full of prophetic fire, and his whole figure wild and lost in his irresistible emotion, stood a workman of the people. His words flashed like the lightning, and struck. From the chief engineer, to his lowest servant, that lawless cry had instant obedience. Water was dashed upon the cables; they bit fiercely into the granite; the windlasses were manned once more: the obelisk rose to its place, and took its stand for centuries.

"It is well that there is order, and discipline, and law; and even the pain of death, perhaps, for their sake; for the divine man, when God sends him, is not stopped by death, in that he bears life eternal, and the feeling of it, in his breast." By law, controlling individual caprice; by individual insight and sympathy and conscience spurning law and self and penalty to the winds together;—Society moves by both to its completeness, the visible temple of the Spirit.

VI. Again, Christianity holds the even balance between the conservation of what is old and the search after and the progress into what is new. It would advance the world without destroying; it would reform constructively; and, only when there is some excess or fatal obstinacy of evil, seize the hammer and the sword, or grow radical enough to lay the axe to the root of the social institutions. Its chosen emblems are the sunlight, the leaven, the mustard-seed, the wheat; where no angry violence quarrels with the opposing element. It would overturn and cast off, just as the up-pushing and vital energy of the opening germ casts aside the old shell that gives up its inner life to a nobler and fairer form. What is good it keeps, and never suffers to die. What is bad it would so kill that the good shall take no damage from the conflict.

And this, too, is exactly the law of reformation that Society itself prescribes and emphasizes. By the silent or louder exercise of its own inherent forces, it is forever dropping off its worn-out shapes, and dress, and institutions, and clothing itself in a body better suited to the wants and the work of its age. Thus the principles of its steady progression are precisely the principles of the New Testament. It is still the sphere of the Christian ideas. Those ideas are, in fact, the needed guide, safeguard, and steady impulse of its headway. Reform without Christianity is wild, bitter, barren, and soon reactionary and retrogressive. Christianity without reform is a corruption and a falsehood. Accordingly, whenever any great hope stirs in the breast of farsighted and aspiring believers, for social redemption from any terrible and flagrant wrong, you find their souls kindle and burn with the anticipation of a speedy coming of the Son of man. It was so in the apostolic age. It has been so ever since. By a natural relation of things, the emancipation of Society is identified with a fresh enthronement of the Messiah.

So, in utterances resounding as a litany, prayed the noble soul of John Milton, in the troubled times of the English nation, when the freedom of the Commonwealth loomed a little out of the despotism of the Stuarts. "O Thou, the ever-begotten light and perfect image of the Father, intercede! Who is there that cannot trace thee now, in thy beamy walk through the midst of thy sanctuary, amidst those golden candlesticks which have long suffered a dimness? Come, therefore, O Thou that hast the seven stars in thy right hand, appoint thy chosen priests to minister before thee, and duly to press and pour out the consecrated oil into thy holy and ever-burning lamps. And as thou didst dignify our fathers' days with many revelations above all the foregoing ages, since thou tookest the flesh, so the power of thy grace is not passed away with the primitive times, but *thy kingdom is now at hand*, and thou standing at the door. Come forth out of the royal chambers, O Prince of all the kings of the earth! Put on the visible robes of thy imperial majesty; for now the voice of thy bride calls thee, and all creatures sigh to be redeemed!"

So, too, entreats the spirit of Channing, standing on the confines between this life and the next, the shadows already stealing down over the eyes that had gazed forward for the emancipation of the American slave,—at the climax of his last appeal for that Christian jubilee: "O come, thou kingdom of heaven, for which we daily pray! Come, Friend and Saviour of the race, who didst shed thy blood on the cross, to reconcile man to man, and earth to heaven! Come, ye predicted ages of righteousness and love, for which the faithful have so long yearned! Come, Father Almighty, and crown with thine Omnipotence the humble strivings of thy children to subvert oppression and wrong, to spread light and freedom, peace and joy, the truth and spirit of thy Son, through the whole earth!"

Society protests against the abuses and the injuries and the bigotries that mortal passions try to foist upon mankind, in the holy name of Nazareth. It insists that religion is for man, as man is for God; that the Church is for Society, as Society is for Christ; that the body is always for the spirit, and never the spirit for the body. The question it ever asks is, Dost thou bless the family of man? If not, thou didst not come from God.

There are two churches in Christendom; one the church of class-privilege, of a priestly caste,—aristocratic, dogmatic, anti-social. The name of that is a Hierarchy. The other is a church of common sentiments, of popular benefaction, — republican, charitable, social. The name of that is a Brotherhood.

VII. Finally, central to the life and power of Christ's religion is the idea of voluntary suffering to save others. Pain, sorrow, wrong and sin are in the world, tragical and portentous shapes. Often solitary in their dark visitation,—each soul tasting of the bitter cup alone, no stranger intermeddling with the grief,—yet they are social shadows also; and by their wonderful working on the disinterested affections and the nobler sympathies these terrible avengers put on the beauty of heaven, and the phantoms of despair are changed into the angels of deliverance.

"I know, is all the sufferer saith,
Knowledge by suffering entereth,
And Life is perfected by Death."

One look into the homes of men will be enough; nor will it matter much what home you choose, so faithful and so universal is that ministry. Is it not the common-place of all domestic speech, where sickness and strangerhood come together, that we never know, till we are troubled, how friendly the human heart is, and how kindness keeps its dwelling-place, firm and warm, even among all the icebergs of selfishness and distrust that chill and chafe the inner sea? Everywhere sorrow melts away the frost; everywhere pale cheeks and aching limbs are apostles of mercy, and regenerators of avarice; everywhere affliction and misery break through reserve, and turn the colder side of human hearts to the sun; everywhere "orphanage is spiritual panoply," tears soften pride, anguish unlocks timidity, the coffin is a signal for compassion, and pain proclaims anew, "Peace on earth, good will to men." Take away suffering from humanity, and you bereave the world of how much of its spiritual glory!

More than this; and diviner glory than this: it is in the heart of humanity,—the divinest thing there,—that suffering should be freely and vicariously undertaken, to save some other from suffering. Love is equal to that; and only they who never loved need to have it proved. Parents and children, brothers and sisters, lovers and friends, oh! what burdens,—how secret, how hard, how bitter,—they are bearing, in all these houses around us, in many of these breasts among us here, to save one another something! It is a law that touches every form of life with sacred splendor. In millions of lesser Gethsemanes love prays, and agonizes, and takes up its lighter crosses, for love's dear sake. Frailty expends its remaining strength to hide its kindred's shame. Mothers watch the stars out for ungrateful children. The friend begs to die for his friend. The missionary leaves home, health, life, for the brother he longs to rescue. The highest patriotism, heroism, martyrdom, is vicarious sacrifice. Literature glows with it; eloquence is vocal with it; music chants it; monuments commemorate it; the aspiring thoughts of the world glory in it.

Nay, so manifestly would the Maker bind all together in bonds of mutual care, and make sacrifice and responsibility keep pace together, that very often this social suffering is made involuntary and inevitable. The crime of one casts gloom and wretchedness upon an innocent household. Rash or unprincipled men ruin their partners or employers in business. The carelessness of a railway conductor plunges a hundred lives into destruction, and scatters misery through a land. In countless ways, we have to be hindered, baffled, sufferers for other men's sins. It is the law of the social constitution, gracious, beautiful in its awfulness. If one member suffer, all the members suffer, not only with it, but *may* suffer for it.

We approach the world's one holiest spot; we bow towards Calvary; and this universal law of the race finds at once its crowning example and its complete interpretation. In its illustrative and affecting light, we read again, and with a more understanding heart, how our salvation does indeed stand in him,—"The Lamb that was slain from the foundation of the world." There was One, great enough, holy enough, disinterested enough, divine enough to be a Sacrifice—not for kindred, not for neighbors, not for countrymen, but for all, of all time, that will believe it. All the old imagery of altars, and the emblems and types of Hebrew sacrifice, grow simple and significant. Every hour of our own sympathetic grief, so dark in itself, holds a lamp of burning lustre over that mysterious text,—"Christ, our passover, is sacrificed for us." The inmost fact of Society, the inmost fact of Christianity, meet and are one. The cross redeems humanity; humanity cries out for the cross, till the hour has come, and then raises its thanksgivings for it, till the latest hour of time. And from all the tongues, and tribes, and generations, and countries, and centuries, from "the multitude that no man can number," goes up the anthem, "Worthy is the Lamb that was slain, to receive power, and riches, and wisdom, and strength, and honor, and glory, and blessing."

My friends, who have patiently followed on with me through these serious studies, we can ascend no higher than this: we can catch no more heavenly note. We can press no closer into the deep heart of our theme. Here we must rest, and part. We have found the answer to the world's profoundest want;—the interpreter of all the meaning and the mystery of the whole historic drama from the beginning to the end;—the law within and above all other laws, for the final destiny of Society, in the person of its Head and its Lord, Emmanuel, God with us.

There the fallen, erring, stumbling race is reconciled again to its Father. There Society confesses its faith. There law and love unite. There mercy and justice embrace each other. There earth and heaven meet.

How can I better or more briefly recall the chief topics I have touched, than by simply naming their bearing on this ultimate and worthy destination of them all? Human Society manifests the Power, the Wisdom, and the Goodness of our God.

First, By its origin, its constitution, its growth, it clearly stands the divine appointment, in itself, of the Father of Christ. Secondly, By the ideas it embodies, it is one visible expression of "the Word that was in the beginning with God," "by whom he made the worlds." Thirdly, It is, in its whole structure, relations, and workings, a discipline of individual character,—and character is the immortal fruit of the Spirit. Fourthly, It is a school of mutual help; and service, out of a heart of love, is the grand action of Christian faith. Fifthly, It proceeds, by natural methods, which artificial arrangements cannot permanently hurry nor retard, in a sublime movement of Providence. Sixthly, It is a motive and an incentive to the human intellect; and the consecrated mind is the noblest workman of the truth. Seventhly, It is ever progressive, in the sweep and the drift of its moral forces: and so it is a fit body for that inexhaustible and unresting spirit which reaches forth unto the things that are before, and seeks to be perfect as the Father in heaven is perfect. Eighthly, It opens the appropriate sphere, and gradually takes the symmetrical and celestial form, of the kingdom of Christ on earth.

What, then, though in its weakness and ignorance, its sensuality and shame, its superstition, starvation and slavery, its selfish riches, and unjust power, and crawling meanness, and unbelieving lust, and unhallowed toil, the social creation, in so many fields and cities of the fair world, travaileth and groaneth in pain together until now, waiting for the manifestation of the sons of God? The voice still crieth in that wilderness, "Prepare ye the way of the Lord. Make straight in that desert a highway for our God. Every valley shall be exalted, and every mountain and hill shall be brought low, and the crooked shall be made straight, and the rough places plain; and the glory of the Lord shall be revealed." There is the consummation; not human, but divine.

Among the splendid visions of a Hebrew prophet, was one vision of living creatures, moving on wheels of fire, bearing up the eternal throne. Whither the Spirit was to go, the winged creatures went; and they turned not when they went. When the living creatures were lifted up, the wheels were lifted up; and the noise of their wings was as the voice of the Almighty.

The world is waiting for a realization of the vision. Into the myriad wheels of the living social system,—wheels within wheels,—is to come the living Spirit from on high, flooding them with the holy radiance of truth, overshadowing them with its wings of peace, moving them when it moves, lifting them up when it ascends, by its benignant and omnipotent will. Then they will bear on, over the highways that Christian toil has cast up, the church and cross of God's love, conquering the deserts of suffering and sin with the gentleness and sunshine of the morning.

"I saw the holy city, new Jerusalem, and I heard a great voice out of heaven; Behold, the tabernacle of God is with men, and he will dwell with them, and they shall be his people, and God himself shall be with them."

"As wheeled by seeing spirits toward the East,
* * * * where faint and fair,
Along the tingling desert of the sky,
Beyond the circle of the conscious hills,
Were laid, in jasper-stone, as clear as glass,
The first foundations of that new, near Day
Which should be builded out of heaven to God!
* * * * 'Jasper first,' I said,
'And second, sapphire; third, chalcedony;
The rest in order; last, an amethyst.'"

THE END.

UNIFORM WITH THIS VOLUME.

GRAHAM LECTURES.

FIRST SERIES.

THE

CONSTITUTION OF THE HUMAN SOUL.

BY

RICHARD S. STORRS, Jr., D.D.

8vo. $1 75.

NEW BOOKS.

A. L. O. E. Series.
8 vols. 18mo, each, ... 50
4 " " " 30
5 " " " 25
Anna; or, a Daughter at Home, 50
Baillie's Life Studies. 18mo, . 40
Life of St. Augustine, . . . 75
Life of Capt. Bate, ... 75
Beautiful Home. 18mo, . . 30
Bonar's Land of Promise, . 1 25
Bonar on the Psalms, . . 1 75
Bunbury's Fanny the Flower Girl, 30
Butler's Lectures on Revelation,
Brook Farm, ... 60
Brooke on Dancing, ... 30
Breckinridge, Rev. Robt., D.D.
The Knowledge of God Objectively Considered, ... 2 00
Do. Subjectively Considered, . . 2 50
Bunyan, John.
Pilgrim's Progress. 20 Large Plates, 1 00
Cabell's Unity of Mankind, 1 00
Caird's Sermons, ... 1 00
Cooke's
Memories of My Life Work, . . 1 00
Cottage and its Visitor, . . . 60
Duff's Indian Rebellion, . . 75
Eadie on Philippians, . . 2 00
Paul the Preacher, ... 1 25
Ellie Randolph, ... 75
First and Last Journey, . . . 40
English Hearts and Hands, . . 75
Gallaudet's Memoir, . . . 1 00
Gatty's Circle of Blessings, . . 30
Motes in Sunbeam, ... 30
World Not Realized, . . . 30
Proverbs. Illustrated, . . . 30
Alice and Adolphus, . . . 50
Parables from Nature, . . . 50
Aunt Judy's Tales, ... 50
Griscom's Life, ... 2 00
Guinness' Sermons, . . . 1 00
Guthrie, Rev. Thos., D.D.
The Saint's Inheritance, . . . 1 00
The City; Its Sins and Sorrows, . 50
Hamilton, Rev. James, D.D.
Sacred Classics. 4 vols, . . . 4 00
Life of James Wilson. . . . 1 00
Hall's, Newman.—Now, . . 25
Hammond's Life, . . . 1 00
Havelock's Life, ... 1 00
Hodge on 2d Corinthians, . 1 00
Huntington's Human Society, 1 75
Jacobus on Acts, . . . 1 00
James' Christian Hope, . . . 75

Julia, The $1 00
Kate and Effie, ... 50
Lays of the Holy Land, . 3 50
Lectures to Young Men, . 1 00
Leighton's Works. 8vo, . 2 00
Lewis' Divine Human, . . 1 00
Light for the Line, ... 25
Little Lychetts, ... 75
Lillie on the Thessalonians, . .
Macduff's
Memories of Gennesaret, . . . 1 00
Child's Book of Divinity, . . 25
Bow in the Cloud, ... 40
Story of Bethlehem, ... 60
Hart and the Water Brooks, . 60
Malan's Magdala and Bethany, . 40
Mendip Annals, ... 60
Mia and Charlie, ... 50
Ministering Children. Illust., 1 00
Missing Link, ... 75
Monod's Farewell, ... 50
Murdock's
Mosheim's Eccles. History. 3 vols., 6 00
Trans. of Syriac Testament, . . 2 00
Newton's Best Things, . . . 75
Rills from the Fountain, . . . 75
Passing Clouds, ... 50
Proverbs of Solomon. Illust., 2 50
Race and the Prize, . . . 6
Round the Fire, ... 75
Ryle on Luke. 2 vols., . 2 00
Shadow on the Hearth, . . . 75
Sheepfold and Common. Illust., 1 25
Sidney Grey. Illust., . . . 50
Sprague's
Annals of American Pulpit.
Vols. 1 & 2.—Congregationalists, . 5 00
" 3 & 4.—Presbyterians, . . 5 00
" 5. —Episcopalians, . . 2 50
" 6. —Baptists, . . . 3 00
Sunday Afternoons in Nursery, . 50
Taylor's Life of Christ, . . 2 00
Three Wakings, ... 75
Thomson's Seasons. Illust., 4 50
Tyng's Captive Orphan, . 1 00
Truth Always Best, ... 25
Uncle Jack the Fault Killer, . 30
Unica, by the same Author, . 25
Voice of Christian Life in Song, 75
Warfare and Work. A Tale, 50
Winslow, Mrs. Mary, Life of, 1 00
On Precious Things of God, . . 1 00

Made in the USA
Monee, IL
20 October 2026

66035303R00179